Professional Negligence in Construction

ESSENTIAL READING

Dictionary of Property and Construction Law
Edited by J. Rostron, co-edited by L. Wright, L. Tatham and R. Hardy-Pickering
Spon Press
Hbk 0–419–26100–1
Pbk 0–418–26110–9

Construction Contracts third edition
John Murdock and Will Hughes
Spon Press
Hbk: 0–419–26170–2
Pbk: 0–419–25310–6
eBook: 0–203–18498–X

Understanding the JCT Standard Building Contracts seventh edition
David Chappell
Spon Press
Pbk: 0–415–30631–0

Understanding the Building Regulations second edition
Simon Polley
Spon Press
Pbk: 0–419–24720–3

Information and ordering details
For price availability and ordering visit our website **www.sponpress.com**
Alternatively our books are available from all good bookshops.

Professional Negligence in Construction

Ben Patten

Spon Press
Taylor & Francis Group

LONDON AND NEW YORK

First published 2003
by Spon Press
11 New Fetter Lane, London EC4P 4EE

Simultaneously published in the USA and Canada
by Spon Press
29 West 35th Street, New York, NY 10001

Spon Press is an imprint of the Taylor & Francis Group

© 2003 Ben Patten

Typeset in Sabon by
Keystroke, Jacaranda Lodge, Wolverhampton
Printed and bound in Great Britain by MPG Books Ltd, Bodmin

British Library Cataloguing in Publication Data
A catalogue record for this book is available from the British Library

Library of Congress Cataloging-in-Publication Data
Patten, Ben.
    Professional negligence in construction / Ben Patten.
      p. cm.
    Includes index.
    ISBN 0–415–29066–X (hardback)
    1. Architects—Malpractice—Great Britain. 2. Consulting engineers—
    Malpractice—Great Britain. 3. Construction contracts—Great Britain.
    I. Title.
    KD2978.P38 2003
    343.41′078624—dc21   2003000172

Contents

Acknowledgments

The author and the publishers are grateful to the Royal Institute of British Architects for permission to reproduce as Appendix 1 the APIA–RIBA 2002 policy wording and as Appendix 2 the Conditions of Engagement from the Standard Form of Agreement SFA/99. They are also grateful to the Association of Consulting Engineers for permission to reproduce as Appendix 3 section B of the Association's Conditions of Engagement agreement A (1) 2002. Appendix 4, RICS Form of Agreement and Terms and Conditions of the Appointment of a Quantity Surveyor, from *Appointing a Quantity Surveyor*, is reproduced by permission of the Royal Institute of Chartered Surveyors, which owns the copyright.

Introduction

This book is concerned with the liabilities of construction professionals and in particular architects, engineers, quantity surveyors, project managers, claims consultants and experts. It is intended to be a practical guide, which, although it seeks to explain relationships that are ultimately matters of law, is primarily intended for the non-lawyer.

The precise meaning of the term 'professional' probably depends upon the point of view of the person using it. Most builders would consider themselves to be professionals in one sense in which that word is understood. Indeed given that 'unprofessional' is commonly used as a term of denigration, it might be difficult to find any person carrying out any form of employment in which he or she takes pride who would not regard themselves as 'professional.' However, 'a professional' in the sense that sociologists and lawyers might understand that phrase, connotes a person whose work and attitudes contain particular characteristics: the work itself is generally skilled and specialised, mental rather than manual and usually the product of training and even examination rather than experience; there is an expectation that professionals are committed to a work ethic which requires them to aspire to a high standard of performance for its own sake and not just the requirements of the particular contract; they commonly belong to collective organisations which prescribe rules of conduct and set common standards; lastly they aspire to and receive a status in the eyes of their fellows – a professional status.[1] At root public perception is perhaps the most important of these ingredients. In *Carr* v. *IRC*[2] Lord Justice DuParq stated:

> It seems to me to be very dangerous to try to define the word 'profession.' I think that everybody would agree that, before once can say a man is carrying on a profession, one must see that he has some special skill or ability or some special qualification derived from training or experience.

1 I am indebted to the learned editors of *Jackson and Powell on Professional Negligence*, fifth edition, for this analysis.
2 [1944] 2 AER 163.

Even then one has to be very careful, because there are many people whose work demands great skill and ability and long experience and many qualifications who would not be said by anybody to be carrying on a profession. Ultimately one has to ask this question: Would the ordinary man, the ordinary reasonable man . . . say now, in the time in which we live, of any particular occupation, that it is properly described as a profession? Times have changed. There are professions today which nobody would have considered to be professions in times past. Our forefathers restricted the professions to a very small number; the work of the surgeon used to be carried out by a barber, whom nobody would have considered a professional man. The profession of chartered accountant has grown up in comparatively recent times, and other trades, or vocations . . . may in future years acquire the status of professionals.

Indeed the term 'construction professional' has no very precise meaning. The construction industry employs many different types of professional person including not just architects, engineers, quantity surveyors, project managers, claims consultants and experts but also lawyers and accountants. However, the scope of this book is confined to those professions whose core activities are concerned with construction.

'Liability' is a legal term and whilst this is not intended to be a book for lawyers, it is inevitably a book which contains a lot of law. Chapter 1 sets out the legal framework within which the liabilities of construction professionals can be understood. It examines the central role of the professional's contract with his client and the ancillary role of his tortious duties both to his client and third parties. The duty to take 'reasonable skill and care' is considered and the meaning of that phrase is explained. The way in which the courts establish what compensation flows from any particular breach of duty is discussed as are the restrictions which are imposed upon the types of loss that will be compensated. Lastly, I examine some of the particular rules that operate to restrict or extend potential liability – such as limitation and contribution proceedings.

Chapter 2 deals with one of the most important practical considerations affecting all construction professionals, namely professional indemnity insurance. The reality of nearly every professional negligence action taken against construction professionals is that behind the professional stands his professional indemnity insurer and it is that insurer who will dictate the conduct of the professional's defence. I discuss the ways in which professional indemnity policies operate, the respective rights of insurer and insured and the ways that insurers operate in practice when organising the defence of a professional who has had a claim made against him. At Appendix 1 I have reproduced by way of example the policy wording from the professional indemnity policy used by most architects.

Chapter 3 is concerned with architects and engineers, both professions being taken together on account of the similarity in their liabilities. Standard contractual obligations are discussed and I examine of the types of breach of duty which are most frequently alleged, together with consideration of how such cases are considered by the courts and what factors will and will not point towards a finding of breach of duty. At Appendices 2 and 3 I have reproduced the terms and conditions of two of the most commonly used contracts for architects and engineers, namely the Royal Institute of British Architects' Standard Form of Appointment (SFA/99) and the Association of Consulting Engineers' Conditions of Engagement Agreement A (1).

Chapter 4 is about quantity surveyors. I explain the construction industry functions generally undertaken by this profession and how the duty to take reasonable care and skill is applied to some of these activities. At Appendix 3 I have reproduced the Form of Agreement and Terms of Appointment produced by the Royal Institute of Chartered Surveyors.

Chapters 5 and 6 concern relatively new 'professions' within the construction industry, namely project managers, claims consultants and expert witnesses. One of the striking changes in the industry over the last thirty years has been the increasing complexity of the tasks it undertakes and the proliferation of different specialists whose job it is to carry out these tasks. Project managers – whose function is to manage these specialists – are a direct response to that complexity. Claims consultants and expert witnesses are in part also a direct response to the complexity of modern construction projects but are also the product of the increasing number and value of disputes arising from construction projects.

Lastly, in Chapter 7 I discuss the ways in which construction disputes are resolved in practice. In particular this involves an examination of alternative dispute resolution which has become increasingly important over the last decade as a means of resolving disputes involving construction professionals. However, I also consider adjudication, arbitration and of course litigation, all of which have undergone significant change in recent times.

Inevitably a book like this runs a number of risks. The first of these is over-simplification. It cannot be stressed too highly that each professional negligence action involving a construction professional will be decided on the basis of its individual facts and it would be unsafe to draw hard-and-fast conclusions in relation to any practical problem from the illustrations provided in this book: they can do no more than provide a very general guide. Secondly, in what is a very rapidly changing legal environment there is always the risk that new decisions by the courts or new legislation will make some statements of law unreliable. In general this is unlikely as I have done my best to elucidate settled principles and to avoid describing the state of the law in areas where it is fluid. However, it should none the less be noted that this book reflects the law as at October 2002.

1 The legal framework

In order to understand the nature of the legal duties which construction professionals owe to their clients and to other persons, it is necessary to know something of the general law of contract and tort. Similarly in order to appreciate the extent to which any particular professional might be held liable to pay damages to a client or some other person it is necessary to understand the broad outlines of the ways in which the law deals with issues of causation and compensation. Moreover in order to judge whether a professional may be at risk in a claim and the extent of that risk it is further necessary to have in mind some of the special rules which the law has devised both to enable certain kinds of claims to be made and to prevent certain kinds of claims being made in certain circumstances. This chapter is addressed to all construction professionals although so far as possible practical examples are employed to illustrate the points made.

Contractual duties

In almost all cases of professional negligence disputes between construction professionals and their clients the extent of the professional's legal obligations to the client are governed by his contract with the client. The contract is the legal agreement by which the professional and his client agree their respective rights and obligations. It may contain express provisions which set out those rights and obligations relevant to the particular dispute. Alternatively, if the contract is silent as to these obligations, the law will treat them as being implied. Once a contract exists – no matter how rudimentary – it will almost certainly be the main point of reference for judging the obligations which the professional owed to his client. Most professional organisations produce standard contracts, examples of which are to be found in the appendices. However, by no means every construction professional contracts with his client on the basis of these standard contracts and indeed some contract on the basis of no written documents at all. Even a conversation in which the professional agrees with the client that he will undertake work for a reasonable fee will constitute a contract. Sometimes the parties agree that the professional will undertake work on precise terms to be agreed later. Some time after the work has commenced the parties may sign a formal contract which has effect from the commencement of the work. In other instances the parties may agree that the professional will carry out work with an implicit agreement that his contract will be governed by certain standard terms or even custom and practice. Once two persons have made an agreement of a commercial nature the courts are reluctant not to treat it as a contract and if one participant to the agreement tries to persuade a court that he had no intention to create a binding contract he will generally face an uphill struggle.

Most disputes involving construction professionals, although they may also be concerned with the professional's alleged failure to comply with very specific terms of the contract, are concerned with a more general failure by the professional to exercise 'reasonable skill and care'. Thus, the surveyor who miscalculates the estimated cost of a project, thereby encouraging the client to believe that it will be cheaper than was really the case, is likely to be in breach of his contractual obligation to use reasonable skill and care rather than any specific express term as to the way in which he carries out calculations. Similarly the architect who produces a faulty design for a factory floor where the screed and toping are inadequate to withstand the usual wear and tear which the floor can be expected to sustain is likely to be in breach of his contractual obligation to use reasonable skill and care rather than any specific express term as to the way in which he specifies the flooring.

Most standard form contracts produced by the construction professional's professional bodies contain an express term which stipulates that the professional will carry out his duties using reasonable skill and care. Thus the RIBA Standard Form of Agreement for the Appointment of an Architect (SFA/99) sets out at condition 2.1:

> The Architect shall in performing the Services and discharging all the obligations under this Part 2 of these Conditions, exercise reasonable skill and care in conformity with the normal standards of the Architect's profession.

Similarly the Association of Consulting Engineers Conditions of Engagement Agreement AI states at condition 2.3:

> The Consulting Engineer shall exercise reasonable skill, care and diligence in the performance of the Services.

The RICS Form of Agreement for use with the RICS Terms and Conditions for the Appointment of a Quantity Surveyor at clause 1.1 states that:

> The Quantity Surveyor shall perform the Services with reasonable skill, care and diligence.

Most bespoke written contracts will contain similar wording. Of course it is open to the parties to attempt to agree that the professional shall perform his services to a higher standard. One way of doing this is to agree a warranty of performance (see below). Another is to include an obligation which attempts to impose some higher degree of skill and care. This is sometimes seen in the use of phrases such as 'utmost skill and care' and 'highest degree of skill and care.' However, it is very difficult to judge in practical terms what these phrases actually mean and usually they are held by the courts to be no more onerous than the familiar obligation of reasonable skill and care. Where the obligation to use reasonable skill and care is not expressly stated in a contract the courts will none the less treat the contract as containing that obligation. Whilst the provision is now implied by Section 13 of the Supply of Goods and Services Act 1982, the law has always regarded such an obligation as implicit in the contractual relationship between any professional man and his client.

Of course some disputes involving construction professionals concern an allegation that the professional failed to carry out a specific act expressly required by his contract. For example if an architect is expressly required to issue certain certificates during the course of construction works pursuant to the terms of the building contract and neglects to do so he is likely to be in breach of a specific contractual term. If an architect gives instructions to a contractor without authority he is likely to be in breach of his obligation to act within his the scope of the authority provided to him rather than his obligation to exercise reasonable skill and care. Similarly if an engineer is expressly required to carry out a certain test or employ a particular method of calculation and he omits to do so he is likely to be in breach of a specific contractual term. Indeed the law will go further and may imply other ancillary obligations in the contract between a professional and his client if the situation demands it. As Oliver J pointed out in *Midland Bank Trust Co. Ltd.* v. *Hett Stubbs & Kemp*,[1] when considering a complaint by a client that a professional engaged by him has failed to perform his duty it may be necessary to look further than a mere obligation to act with reasonable skill and care:

> The classical formulation of the claim in this sort of case as 'damages for negligence and breach of professional duty' tends to be a mesmeric phrase. It concentrates attention on the implied obligation to devote to the client's business that reasonable care and skill to be expected from a normally competent and careful practitioner as if that obligation were not only a compendious, but also an exhaustive, definition of all the duties assumed under the contract created by the retainer and its acceptance. But of course, it is not. A contract gives rise to a complex of

1 [1979] Ch 384.

rights and duties of which the duty to exercise reasonable skill and care is but one. If I employ a carpenter to supply and put up a good quality oak shelf for me, the acceptance by him of that employment involves the assumption of a number of contractual duties. He must supply wood of an adequate quality and it must be oak. He must fix the shelf. And he must carry out the fashioning and fixing with the reasonable care and skill which I am entitled to expect of a skilled craftsman. If he fixes the brackets but fails to supply the shelf or if he supplies and fixes a shelf of unseasoned pine, my complaint against him is not that he has failed to exercise reasonable care and skill in carrying out the work but that he has failed to supply what was contracted for.

By agreeing to exercise reasonable skill and care in the performance of his work the construction professional is not usually also agreeing that he will achieve a particular result. The architect who agrees to designs a building does not at the same time agree that the design will work. He commits himself to using reasonable skill and care in providing that design and it may be that the fact that the design does not work is strong prima facie evidence that he did not exercise that reasonable skill and care. However, the mere fact of a failure of design is not of itself a breach of duty. Similarly an engineer who agrees to provide structural calculations to enable the design of the foundations of a building to be completed does not at the same time agree that the calculations will be accurate in the sense that the foundations will be adequate. It may be that because of matters he could not have known about, for example some quirk in the ground conditions which was not apparent on the basis of the surveys and soil tests, the foundations needed to be deeper or wider and accordingly failed to perform notwithstanding the fact that the surveyor exercised reasonable skill and care. As HH Judge Seymour QC said in *Royal Brompton Hospital NHS Trust* v. *Hammond No. 7*:[2]

> All of this does, of course, emphasise the vital point that the duty of a professional man, generally stated, is not to be right, but to be careful. While, unless in a particular case, the professional man is actually wrong, the fact that he has not been careful will probably not cause his client any loss, the fact that he is in the event proved to be wrong is not, in itself, any evidence that he has been negligent. His conduct is to be judged having regard to all the information available to him, or which ought to have been available to him, at the time he gave his advice or made his decision or did whatever else it is that he did.

There are exceptions to this distinction. The architect may expressly agree that his design will be successful. The engineer may expressly agree that the foundations designed according to his calculations will be adequate. However, such 'warranties' are relatively rare for obvious reasons. In making such agreements the architect or the engineer would be guaranteeing the success of the design notwithstanding that factors outside of their control might lead the design to be unsuccessful. Very occasionally the courts have suggested that in certain situations persons who undertake certain professional work do indeed agree to such onerous obligations. In *IBA* v. *EMI and BICC*[3] Lord Scarman said that 'one who contracts to design an article for a purpose made known to him undertakes that the design is reasonably fit for its purpose.' However, there has been a marked judicial reluctance to apply such stringent obligations to the contracts of construction professionals and as a rule of thumb it is safe to say that, in the absence of a specific agreement that a certain result will be achieved, the duty of the construction professional to his client is to exercise reasonable skill and care.

Lastly it should be noted that although the foregoing analysis has dealt with contractual duties owed to a client as a result of an agreement, it is possible that a construction professional may owe contractual duties to a person who was not his client, or at least not his original client, by the process of *novation* or by the provision of a collateral warranty. In novation a third person agrees that he will step into the shoes of the client in terms of the client's agreement with the professional. By so doing he takes on the benefits and burdens of the contract as if he had been the client from the outset. Typically, a substantial construction project may require the contractor to design and build the works having made use of a preliminary design produced by the client's architect. The client's architect will have previously produced the design pursuant to a contract entered into with the client. The construction contract makes the contractor responsible for the entirety of the design and it is agreed between the parties that on signing the construction contract the contractor will be novated to the architect's contract of appointment and will thus step into the shoes of the client. In this way the duty to take reasonable care and skill which the architect undertook to the client is transformed into being a duty to take reasonable care and skill owed to the contractor, even though the work was carried out at time before the contractor had any dealings with the architect. By contrast a collateral warranty is a separate agreement entered into between a construction professional and a third person by which the construction professional agrees in return for a fee (usually nominal) to owe certain duties to the third person. These duties are usually the same or similar to the duties which he owes to his client. Typically an employer will engage a contractor on a design and build contract which contemplates that the contractor will appoint an engineer (under a subcontract) to design certain structural parts of the works. The design-and-build contract will require the contractor to ensure that the engineer enters

3 [1980] 14 BLR 1.

into a collateral warranty[4] with the employer in respect of the design works whereby the engineer agrees to owe a duty to the employer to carry out his design works with reasonable skill and care. In this way the employer obtains the additional protection of being able to take legal proceedings against the contractor or the engineer should the latter not carry out his work with reasonable skill and care and the works be defective as a result.

Tortious duties

Tortious liability in the field of professional negligence can be broadly described as the right of a person who has suffered damage, as a result of the negligence of a professional person in the way he carried out his work, to recover compensation from that professional person. It operates irrespective of contractual relationships (although these may be present) and is largely the creation of judicial precedent. The tort of negligence is complete – that is, the person who has suffered damage may sue – when the following three conditions are satisfied:

1 The professional owes a 'duty of care' to that person.
2 The professional has acted in such a way as to break that duty of care (usually by failing to exercise reasonable skill and care in the way he carried out his work).
3 That person has suffered relevant damage as a result of the breach of duty.

The most obvious circumstance in which a professional owes a duty of care to another person is if that person has contracted with him. In this situation the tortious duty of care and the contractual duties run in parallel.[5] Indeed whilst it is possible that the tortious duty may in rare circumstances be less extensive than the contractual duty, it can never be more onerous because it is the 'proximity' provided by the contractual relationship which gives rise to the duty of care in the first place and its scope is to be construed according to the scope of the contractual obligations. It follows that, whilst in the usual case a construction professional who fails to exercise reasonable skill and care when working for his client (which results in the client suffering loss) will be in breach of *both* contractual and tortious duties, the existence of the tortious duty adds nothing of substance to the merits of the client's case. In practical terms, although construction professionals who are sued by their clients are invariably sued in contract and in tort, there is

---

4 Some professional bodies – for example the RICS – recommend the use of specific forms of collateral warranty designed to offer as much protection to the professional as is likely to be commercially acceptable.
5 *Henderson v. Merrett Syndicates Ltd* [1995] 2 AC 145.

no difference between either cause of action and the tortious breach adds nothing. This is subject to one particular exception which concerns limitation periods (see below).

The importance of tortious liability to construction professionals lies not in their relationships with their clients but in their relationships with third parties.

1   An architect is employed by his client to administer a construction contract. He issues certain certificates valuing the works carried out at particular stages. The contractor is aggrieved by these valuations which he believes are substantially below his entitlement. Before the contractor can take action under the building contract against the employer the latter becomes insolvent. Assuming that the valuations were not carried out with reasonable skill and care, can the contractor sue the architect for negligently under-certifying his entitlement?

2   An engineer provides a design for a certain parts of a warehouse to company A. The warehouse is completed according to that design. Company A sells the warehouse to company B. The design is defective as a result of the want of reasonable skill and care on the part of the engineer. Because of the defects the warehouse floods, damaging goods inside. Can company B sue the engineer and can it recover compensation for both the repair of the warehouse and the value of the goods?

3   A contractor is in negotiations with a prospective client who is contemplating building a house. The contractor produces a design but is unable to price the work. He obtains an estimate from a friendly quantity surveyor who knows that both the contractor and his prospective client will rely upon it. The contractor shows the estimate to the prospective client, explaining that he cannot take responsibility for its accuracy but stating that it was produced by the quantity surveyor. Relying on the estimate the prospective client decides that he can afford to build the house and enters into a building agreement with the contractor whereby the latter will be paid a reasonable sum for the work rather than a flat fee. Because of errors made by the quantity surveyor the house is much more expensive to build than was anticipated. The client is unable to find the money and the half-built house deteriorates, becoming more expensive still, and eventually has to be abandoned. Can the client sue the quantity surveyor for the loss and damage he has suffered as a result of the quantity surveyor's failure to carry out his work with reasonable skill and care?

It is right to say that the law in this area is far from straightforward and a full explanation is beyond the scope of this book. However, at the risk of oversimplification, the broad outlines of when a duty of care will be made out are as follows. The first key to establishing that construction professional A owes third party B a duty of care in tort is the 'proximity' between A and

B: in particular, how readily apparent would it have been to A that an error in the way in which he carried out his work might cause 'damage' to B ? The second key is whether it is just and reasonable that there should be a duty of care. Applying these tests the courts in England have largely considered the existence of tortious duty in negligence according to the kind of loss sought to be compensated. Some kinds of damage more readily give rise to a duty of care than others. If construction professional A negligently designs a wall with the consequence that it collapses on and injures B, B will probably be able to make out the existence of a duty of care owed to him by A. This is because the courts have always regarded the causing of *personal injury* as likely to give rise to a remedy against the person who caused it.[6] Similarly if construction professional A designs a wall which collapses on and damages B's car, B will probably be able to make out the existence of a duty of care owed to him by A. Again this is because the courts have always regarded the causing of *damage* to other property as likely to give rise to a remedy against the person who caused it.[7] However, if construction professional A designs a wall which is then purchased by B and subsequently collapses causing only financial loss, B will generally be unable to make out the existence of a duty of care. This is because the courts (at least in England)[8] are reluctant to extend the kind of damage which can be recoverable to what is called 'pure economic loss.'[9] In this case even if the wall can be said to have been damaged by A it was not other property. Rather the reality is that the wall was merely not designed very well and consequently was worth less than B paid for it when he bought it. His loss is thus 'pure economic loss'.

There is a class of circumstances where even pure economic loss is recoverable. Suppose that A has designed a wall and B is subsequently considering purchasing it. B goes to A and asks him whether in his opinion the wall is sound. He does not offer to pay A for this information and there is no contract between the two. A says that he designed the wall and he is confident that it is sound. B purchases the wall and it collapses. Here a duty of care will lie in respect of B's loss. This is because in voluntarily reassuring B to the effect that the wall was sound, A assumed a responsibility towards him to take reasonable care in providing that information.[10] In this example it is the carelessness in providing the information which is the negligence (A should have checked its soundness). However, the original error may constitute the negligence if the facts were slightly different. A designs the wall

---

6 *Clay* v. *A.J. Crump & Sons Ltd* [1964] 1 QB 533.
7 See *Bellefield Computer Services Ltd* v. *E. Turner & Sons Ltd* [2000] BLR 97.
8 The position in Canada, Australia and New Zealand is different. Here pure economic loss can give rise to a tortious duty in negligence in certain circumstances; see *Winnipeg Condominium Corp* v. *Bird Construction Co.* [1995] DLR (4th) 193, *Ingles* v. *Tutaluk Construction Ltd* [2000] 1 SCR (4th) DLR 183, *Pyrenees Shire Council* v. *Day* [1998] 192 CLR 330, *Invercargill City Council* v. *Hamlin* [1996] AC 624.
9 *D&F Estates Ltd* v. *Church Commissioners for England* [1989] 1 AC 177.
10 *Hedley Byrne & Co. Ltd* v. *Heller & Partners Ltd* [1964] AC 465.

in the knowledge that it is to be purchased by B and knowing that C intends to sell the wall to B having advertised it as 'built to the highest standards by A.' Here too A assumes a responsibility to B – he can see that B will rely upon his exercise of skill and care.

The latter class of cases where an assumption of responsibility exists is relevant to construction professionals in the context of those (rare) actions where claimants seek to recover loss and damage in tortious negligence from individuals who worked for limited liability companies rather than the companies themselves. Many construction professionals including architects engineers and surveyors provide their services by way of limited liability companies. When a client complains of professional negligence committed by a professional working in one of those companies he will usually take legal proceedings against the company with whom he has a contractual relationship. However, very occasionally the client will seek to sue the individual professional who, he alleges, failed to carry out his work with reasonable skill and care. When this happens the client is usually concerned that the company is insolvent and/or lacks sufficient insurance cover to meet the claim. By and large such claims have failed in England because the courts have held that it is not just and reasonable that such a duty should exist: the client should rely upon the solvency of the company, not the individual working for it.[11] However, the position is not clear-cut[12] and consequently there is always a risk that a duty of care will be made out in these circumstances.

Lastly it should be noted that in the case of new dwelling houses the law provides a form of statutory tort in the shape of the Defective Premises Act 1972. Section 1 (1) of the Act states:

> A person taking on work for or in connection with the provision of a dwelling (whether the dwelling is provided by the erection or by the conversion or enlargement of a building) owes a duty
>
> (a) if the dwelling is provided to the order of any person, to that person; and
> (b) without prejudice to paragraph (a) above, to every person who acquires an interest (whether legal or equitable) in the dwelling;
>
> to see that the work which he takes on is done in a workmanlike or, as the case maybe, professional manner, with proper materials and so that as regards the work the dwelling will be fit for habitation when completed.

---

11 See *Williams* v. *Natural Health Life Foods Ltd* [1998] 1 WLR 830 at 837B.
12 See *Merrett* v. *Babb* [2001] 3 WLR 1 which concerned an employee working for a surveyors' partnership.

Consequently an architect designing or supervising the construction of a dwelling owes a duty to anyone who later purchases the dwelling to ensure that his work is done in a workmanlike or professional manner. However, it should be noted that in order to be in breach of the duty the failure to ensure that the work is done in a workmanlike or professional manner must cause the dwelling to be unfit for habitation when completed. Consequently a defect which has the result that there is no central heating in the bedrooms does not fall within the Act unless the omission made the rooms so cold that they became unfit for habitation. Moreover because time starts to run for limitation purposes (see below) when the dwelling is completed, the practical consequence is that only recent purchasers of a new dwelling are likely to be able to make use of the Act.

Reasonable skill and care

In the vast majority of cases where allegations of professional negligence are made against construction professionals liability will depend upon whether the professional exercised 'reasonable skill and care'. What does this mean and how does a Judge, who almost certainly will have no qualifications as an architect or an engineer or a surveyor, decide whether this standard has been achieved? The general principles are set out by McNair J in the medical negligence case of *Bolam v. Friern Hospital Management Committee:*[13]

> Where you get a situation which involves the use of some special skill of competence . . . the test is the standard of the ordinary skilled man exercising and professing to have that special skill. A man need not possess the highest expert skill at the risk of being found negligent. It is well established law that it is sufficient if he exercises the ordinary skill of ordinary competent man exercising that particular art.

It follows that the standard to be applied is generally the standard recognised to be good practice in the relevant profession.[14] In practical terms, except where the breach is very clear, the court is almost always guided by the evidence of experts. Thus to take an example, suppose that an architect and an engineer are both being sued in respect of a defective floor which was installed in a factory. Both were involved in the design of the floor but each denies that it was his responsibility to ensure that a particular aspect of

---

13 [1957] 1 WLR 582 at 586.
14 There are a limited number of exceptions to this general principle which apply in rare cases. Generally these are confined to cases where the court is satisfied that there is no logical basis for the body of professional opinion upon which the defendant relies, cases where the expert evidence called is really no more than expressions of what the expert himself would have done and cases where the alleged act of negligence does not require any professional expertise but is a matter of common sense – see *J.D. Williams & Co. Ltd* v. *Michael Hyde & Associates Ltd* [2000] Lloyds Rep PN 823.

that design was appropriate to the proposed use of the floor. The court would hear expert evidence from both parties as to good practice in the professions of architect and engineer and (very probably) the correct approach to be taken by either professional to working with professionals of another discipline. The judge would consider the conflicting expert testimony and decide which he preferred – that is, which was the more cogent and authoritative. Occasionally he will find none of the experts entirely persuasive and will formulate a decision which is somewhere between the positions they adopt. Consequently it will be immediately apparent that expert evidence plays a crucial role in professional negligence actions against professionals and the role and responsibilities of experts are considered in more detail in Chapter 6.

However, it should be noted that in deciding whether a professional exercised reasonable skill and care the court is not merely balancing the views of the professionals whom the parties have called to give expert evidence. There are well established considerations which govern the meaning of reasonable skill and care. The first of these is that the professional is not judged upon his actual expertise but the expertise of an ordinarily competent member of his profession. Consequently a trainee quantity surveyor who carries out some of the functions of a quantity surveyor will not generally be judged by the standard of a trainee, but of a qualified and indeed ordinarily experienced quantity surveyor. By the same token, an internationally respected architect will not, in theory, have a higher standard applied to judging the quality of his work than an ordinarily competent architect doing that sort of work. In practice the courts clearly make some allowance for the fact that client who pays for the most highly skilled advice is entitled to expect more than mere competence. Moreover where a construction professional holds himself out as a specialist in a particular field he should be judged by the standards appropriate to a specialist in that field, even if there is nor formal recognition of his specialisation.[15] A further qualification concerns construction professionals working within a larger organisation. The larger and more sophisticated the company or firm within which the individual construction professional works the more likely it is that the courts will regard him as having access to a greater range of expertise and experience. Clearly performing to the standard of the ordinarily competent member of the profession requires the construction professional to keep abreast of the state of professional knowledge relevant to his discipline. In *Eckersly* v. *Binnie & Partners*,[16] in a passage which could be applied equally to any construction professional, Bingham LJ commented on the required standard of performance for consulting engineers thus:

---

15 For further discussion of this difficult area see R.M. Jackson and J.L. Powell, *Professional Negligence* (fifth edition), paras 2–118 and 2–119.
16 (1988) 18 Con LR 1.

A professional man should command the corpus of knowledge which forms part of the professional equipment of the ordinary member of his profession. He should not lag behind other ordinarily assiduous and intelligent members of his profession in knowledge of new advances, discoveries and developments in his field. He should be alert to the hazards and risks inherent in any professional task he undertakes to the extent that other ordinarily competent members of the profession would be alert. He must bring to any professional task he undertakes no less expertise, skill and care than other ordinarily competent members would bring but need bring no more. The standard is that of the reasonable average. The law does not require of a professional man that he be a paragon combining the qualities of polymath and prophet.

It follows that the standard of reasonable skill and care is not fixed. As professions develop new techniques and in particular more effective ways of safeguarding against familiar risks the standard becomes higher. Practices which might have been acceptable and even widely employed as little as ten years ago may now be seen as unreliable and generally inadvisable. It is particularly noteworthy that when considering the standard of reasonable skill and care in the architects and engineers professions regard is frequently had to the body of written guidance current at the time of the alleged breach in the form of professional standards, codes of practice and so forth.

Damages

In almost all legal proceedings where professional negligence is asserted against a construction professional the person pursuing the proceedings is seeking monetary compensation for his losses which is termed *damages*. The fundamental principle underlying the award of damages is to put the injured party in the position he would have been in had the breach of duty not occurred, so far as this can be done by the award of money. However, this principle is itself hedged by other sub-principles and it is worth considering these and the fundamental principle at least in outline in the context of construction professionals.

The first point to note is that the fundamental principle requires the court to establish exactly what loss has been caused by the breach of duty which is not necessarily the same thing as all the 'loss' which the injured person has suffered after the breach of duty arose. The principle of putting the injured party in the position he would have been in had the breach of duty not occurred is sometimes overlooked by persons seeking to claim compensation from construction professionals who may not appreciate the necessity of establishing a strict causal link. For example, a client who has retained an architect to build a house may complain that the architect acted in breach of duty in advising him that no piling works would be required when these were in fact discovered to be necessary shortly before construction commenced.

The client may seek to recover the cost of the piling works from the architect. However, in so doing he omits to apply the fundamental principle. If the breach of duty had not occurred the architect would have advised him that piling works were necessary. He would still have had to pay for them. His true loss is the difference between the position he is now in – very possibly having to pay for the piling works by way of a variation to the building contract – with the position he would have been in – that is, able to include the piling works in the original tender. Similarly a client who complains that a quantity surveyor underestimated the true price of the cost of constructing a building misapplies the fundamental principle if he claims the difference between what the works were estimated to cost and what they did cost. The true loss is the loss of a chance to take a different course of action once the result became apparent.

The fundamental principle has other practical consequences for establishing the true loss that falls to be compensated when a person claims against a construction professional in respect of harm that he has suffered as a result of that professional's breach of duty. Generally speaking the person making the claim – the *claimant* – must show that the loss would not have occurred in any event. For example, suppose that the claimant complains that as a result of the engineer's failure to exercise reasonable skill and care the roof steelwork over a certain part of a factory roof had to be removed and replaced. He will not be able to claim the cost of that removal and replacement if it turns out that because of variations which he instructed, the roof would have had to be redesigned and rebuilt in any event. Similar is true of a claimant who complains that his project manager failed to act with reasonable skill and care when granting a contractor an extension of time because of claimed variations which turned out to be not true variations at all. The claimant would not be able to claim the costs of this extension of time if it turns out that the contractor would have been entitled to and would have sought a similar extension for other reasons in any event. However, an important qualification needs to be added to the statement that the claimant must show that the loss would not have occurred in any event. Quite often a claimant suffers loss as a result of the breaches of duty of two or more persons. They may each argue that the loss would have occurred in any event by reason of the other's breach. However, it would clearly be grossly inequitable if this provided either with a defence and in English law provided that either can be said to have caused the loss, the claimant may recover against that person and leave him to seek a contribution from the other person also responsible. Lastly, it should be noted that when applying the principle the claimant has to give credit for all the benefits he holds as a result of the breach of duty, providing they are true benefits and truly caused by the breach of duty. Thus a claimant who alleges that as a result of his architect's breach of duty he has built a larger and thus more expensive building than was really required may have to give credit for the fact that he now owns a more valuable property than would otherwise have been the case.

The second issue is that not all losses which appear to be caused by the professional's breach of duty will be compensated by an award of damages. Some types of loss may be so distant from the breach of duty that whilst they are certainly the result of the breach of duty they are generally thought to be 'too remote' to permit the courts to make an award of damages. Thus, for example, a breach of duty on the part of an engineer may mean that the client's factory cannot be ready for the date intended. The client may suffer a loss of business. He may also become ill with stress. The costs of the delay, including possibly the loss of business, may be recoverable from the engineer as being the kinds of losses which a reasonable person in his position would have foreseen as being not unlikely consequences of any breach of duty on his part or which otherwise did not arise naturally in the usual course of things as the consequences of such a breach.[17] However, the costs to the client of his illness are unlikely to be recoverable. That form of loss would have seemed so unlikely to a reasonable engineer that it is termed 'too remote' to form the basis of a remedy in damages. Secondly there are some forms of loss where the courts find that the causal relationship with the breach is far from straightforward and that, bearing in mind the nature of the professional's task, his breach of duty cannot be said to have caused the loss.[18] Thus, for example, suppose that an architect is asked to advise upon the likely net lettable space to be made available in a prospective office block development. The architect makes a small but significant miscalculation so that he overestimates the amount of space. Had the true figure been known the client would, on balance, have decided not to proceed with the project. In the event the development proceeds but because of a collapse in the property market the office development is substantially underlet and the client makes a huge loss. A court is likely to find that whilst the architect is liable for some of the loss, he should not be liable for all of it. Bearing in mind the relatively narrow scope of his function – which was to provide information as to net lettable space – he should not be held responsible for the consequences of the client's decision to commence an office development at that stage of the economic cycle.

Most disputes concerning construction professionals involve a claimant seeking a recognised head of loss or damage. These, together with the usual principles applying to proving loss, are set out below.

Costs of rectification

This is the cost of putting right the construction professional's mistake. It is usually the costs of repair or reconstruction. For example, if the project manager fails to ensure a proper transmission of information between the

17 Often referred to as the rule in *Hadley* v. *Baxendale* (1854) 9 Exch 341.
18 *Banque Bruxelles Lambert SA* v. *Eagle Star Insurance Co. Ltd* [1997] AC 191.

architect and the structural engineer with the result that a part of the design is defective, the costs of rectification will be the costs involved in replacing the defectively designed works with works constructed to a satisfactory design. Of course this measure of loss is subject to the overriding principle to put the claimant in the position he would have been in but for the breach of duty. Thus if the design would have been defective in any event (because the structural engineer's calculations were inaccurate) there will be no loss. Similarly if it would have been more expensive to build to the correct design credit will have to be given by the claimant for that increased expense (provided, that is, this would have been a cost to the employer under the original building contract). Moreover the court will not always allow all the costs of repair and reconstruction if that would be disproportionate. In *Ruxley Electronics & Construction Ltd* v. *Forsyth*[19] the contractor was required by his building contract to build a swimming pool with a maximum depth of 7 ft 6 in. In fact he built the pool to a depth of 6 ft. The employer claimed damages equivalent to the costs of reconstructing the pool so as to provide for a maximum depth of 7 ft 6 in. The contractor argued that these costs were disproportionate to the employer's real loss. He provided evidence to the effect that there was no substantial difference in utility between a pool with a maximum depth of 7 ft 6 in. and one with a maximum depth of 6 ft. The judge at first instance rejected the employer's claim that he should be awarded the costs of reconstruction – £21,560 – and instead awarded him damages based on his loss of amenity – £2,500. The case went to the House of Lords, which upheld the judge at first instance.

By contrast, sometimes a claimant will propose to carry out repair works which have the result that he will end up with a more valuable property than would have been the case had the design been correct and the court may allow the claimant to recover this additional benefit. This is called *betterment* and whether the court allows the claimant to recover it will depend upon whether it is necessary to carry out the works to that standard and being the only practicable method of overcoming the consequences of the breach of duty.[20] For example, an engineer may be required to design a foul drainage system for a factory. He may specify an unsuitable material for the drains. Had he specified the right material it would have had a life expectancy of twelve years. After five years the drainage system collapses and the claimant claims the costs of putting in the correct drains. The engineer may object that this will provide the claimant with an unjustified benefit in that he will receive get a brand-new drainage system with a life expectancy of twelve years when had there been no breach of duty the drains would only have a life expectancy of seven years. Whilst the court may be sympathetic to the engineer's argu-

19 [1996] 1 AC 344.
20 See *Richard Roberts Holdings Ltd* v. *Douglas Smith Stimson Partnership and others* (1988) 46 BLR 50.

ment, the claimant is none the less entitled to claim the full costs of the new system if there is no other cheaper system which could be installed and which would provide the claimant with what he had contracted for.

Diminution in value

The second most frequently claimed head of loss in actions involving construction professionals concerns the amount by which the claimant's property is worth less than it should have been worth as a result of the breach of duty and is an alternative to costs of rectification. This basis of valuation is usually applied where the claimant has no intention of carrying out repairs in order to put the property in the condition it should have been in and/or it would be unreasonably expensive to take this course. Thus for example an engineer whose breach of duty may cause the collapse of a property adjacent to the one being restored may be sued for the costs of rebuilding that property or, in the alternative, the difference between the value of that property immediately prior to the collapse and its value after the collapse. If the court decides that the costs of rebuilding are excessive and that that the claimant will probably sell the property rather than rebuild it, it will award the claimant damages based on the diminution in value. However, whilst costs of rectification and diminution in value are usually alternatives they can on occasion be complementary. In our example, suppose that the claimant proposed – and the court found that it was reasonable – that he should carry out a partial restoration of the property before selling the site (in order to make it more attractive to purchasers). The claimant might be awarded both the costs of rectification (or at least partial rectification) and the difference in value between the partially restored property and its value immediately prior to the collapse.[21] A more usual occurrence of this dual award is where a property is completely restored but because of the damage suffers from 'blight' or 'stigma'. In that instance the claimant may recover not merely the costs of rectification but also damages representing the extent to which the property has been made less valuable to potential purchasers.[22]

Wasted expenditure

Wasted expenditure may be claimed as an additional or an alternative head of loss to the kinds of losses identified above. For example, if the project manager fails to ensure a proper transmission of information between the architect and the structural engineer with the result that a part of the design is defective, the claimant's main claim may be the costs of rectification, being

21 See *George Fischer Holding Ltd* v. *Multi Design Consultants Ltd* (1998) 61 Con LR 85 at 145.
22 This may happen in the context of subsidence damage: see *Hoadley* v. *Edwards* [2001] PNLR 41.

the costs involved in replacing the defectively designed works with works constructed to a satisfactory design. However, he may also claim wasted expenditure – for example the costs of obtaining designs and drawings from interior decorators which were based upon the defective design and which cannot now be used for the correct design. Alternatively wasted expenditure may be the only head of claim. Suppose that the project manager's mistake had been discovered long before the construction work was due to start and the only consequence was that the architects had to revise design work under-taken which could be put right easily. In that instance the claimant would claim for the wasted expenditure consisting of the costs of the architect's initial defective design. A claim for wasted expenditure can take the form of a claim of excessive expenditure – for example where an architect has negligently over-certified the value of work and the contractor has thereafter become insolvent so that the value of the overpayment cannot be recovered from it. Alternatively a claim might be made against project managers that by their various acts of mismanagement they had failed to control costs on a project so that the employer had paid the contractor and consultants far more than he needed to.

Consequential losses

There are further types of loss which, although not as immediately caused by the breach of duty as costs of rectification, diminution in value or wasted expenditure, are none the less the consequences of the breach of duty and not too remote or unusual to form the basis of a claim for damages. A structural engineer whose breach of duty resulted in defective foundations for a house may be required to pay damages representing the costs of repair. However, he may also be required to pay damages representing the costs of rehousing the client and his family during the period of those repairs. The architect whose breach of duty led to the roof on a warehouse being inadequately watertight may be required pay damages not just for the costs of repairing the roof, but also in respect of the damage to the client's stock caused by flooding from the roof. A frequently claimed head of consequential loss is the cost of management time devoted to dealing with the problems caused by the breach of duty.

Other types of loss

Although the heads of loss set out above are the most frequently encountered heads of loss in cases involving construction professionals, they are not the only ones. The claimant may have suffered some personal injury which was not too remote a consequence of the professional's breach of duty. The claimant may have suffered inconvenience or may have become vulnerable to a claim by a third party. Sometimes the claimant's loss is really the loss of a chance of achieving some benefit or avoiding some catastrophe and the court has to value that chance as best it can on the basis of all the available evidence.[23] A closely related issue concerns claims by employers that they should be entitled to recover some or all of the fees they paid the professional on the grounds that his breach of duty is so serious that it amounts to non-performance of his contract.[24]

Mitigation

When assessing the loss which a claimant has suffered for the purposes of establishing the amount of damages which a construction professional ought to pay, the court will consider whether the loss would have been smaller had the claimant taken reasonable steps to protect himself. This is often referred to as the claimant's duty to mitigate. In *Board of Governors of Hospitals for Sick Children* v. *McLaughlin & Harvey plc*.[25] Judge Newey QC gave this guidance:

> The [claimant] has, whether as part of the requirement that he act reasonably or otherwise, a duty to mitigate his loss. This may require him if presented with two or more choices to choose the one which will keep his losses to a minimum. If he is incurring loss because he cannot use his property, his duty to mitigate may require him to repair it as quickly as possible, even if early repairs would cost more than later repairs would. The duty to mitigate may require [the claimant] to have regard to advice from third parties, or even from the defendant, or from the defendant's advisers.

Sometimes the costs of repair will be greatly increased if the problem is left unattended until after trial and the court will find that a claimant acting reasonably should have carried out earlier rectification even though he may have been uncertain as to whether he would recover these costs from the construction professional. Alternatively a claimant will be found to have acted unreasonably if he refuses an offer by the professional to correct the mistake for free and instead insists on retaining another professional to carry out the work. However, in each case the court must be satisfied that the claimant has acted unreasonably and will generally have sympathy for the claimant, as the injured party. A claimant of moderate means facing an expensive repair bill and guided by uncertain advice as to how much worse

---

23 This can be a complex exercise, particularly where the value of the lost chance is concerned with the hypothetical actions of third parties – see *J. Sainsbury plc* v. *Broadway Malayan* [1999] PNLR 286, where part of the loss was the loss of a chance that a fire would have been contained if the correct design had been employed.

24 See for example *Turner Page Music Ltd* v. *Torres Design Associates Ltd* [1997] CILL 1263, where the architects' failure to produce a bill of quantities led to the court permitting the recovery of a portion of their fees.

25 (1987) 19 Con LR 25 at 96.

the problem might get is unlikely to be found to have acted unreasonably if he did not immediately incur the costs of repair.

Interest and costs

Whilst the heads of loss identified above illustrate the kinds of awards of damages which may be made against construction professionals, there are two further types of monetary award which a claimant may recover. In the first place the claimant may be awarded interest to compensate him for the loss of use of his money if the award of damages refers to a loss valued at some date prior to trial.[26] Thus if a claimant claims that he has suffered wasted expenditure of, say, £12,000 which he incurred in March of 2001 and which he is awarded at trial in March of 2003, he will usually be awarded two years' interest on that sum (at a rate to be decided by the court). However, if the claimant is claiming the costs of rectification for repair works that have not yet taken place, no interest will be awarded because no expenditure has yet taken place. If successful in his litigation against the defendant or defendants the claimant will usually also be awarded his reasonable legal costs in taking the proceedings. The award of costs is governed by rules of court which are complex.[27] However, by and large costs are awarded to the successful party provided that that party has not behaved unreasonably in the way in which it conducted the litigation. There are special provisions enabling the parties to make use of the threat of costs as an inducement to settle proceedings (see Chapter 7). Moreover because litigation involving construction professionals can be very expensive in terms of legal costs, these are often an important feature and sometimes they are as important as the eventual award of damages.

Limitation

In the usual case whether or not the construction professional is able successfully to defend the proceedings will depend upon whether the claimant can show that professional was in breach of duty and/or whether he can show that the breach of duty caused loss. However, there are two special defences, one a complete defence, the other a partial defence, which the courts make available to defendants. The most important of these is the defence that the claimant's claim is too old to be allowed to be litigated and is 'barred' by the effect of the Limitation Act 1980 which prevents claimants taking claims which originated a certain time before the legal proceedings were commenced. Of particular relevance to construction professionals are Sections 2 and 5 of that Act which prevent claims framed in tort and contract being commenced (1) more than

---

26 The right to interest is almost always afforded under Section 35A of the Supreme Court Act 1981.
27 See parts 44–8 of the Civil Procedure Rules.

six years after damage was suffered, in the case of claims brought in tort and (2) more than six years after the breach of contract, in the case of claims brought in contract. There may be a difference between the date when damage is suffered and the date when the contract is breached and this can mean that actions brought in tort may be within time whereas actions brought in contract are 'barred'. However, the law treats damage as meaning the first occurrence of any meaningful loss or damage, which includes even a relatively modest loss and so often the date of breach of duty and the date when damage occurs will be not too dissimilar. The architect's breach of duty may occur when he provides the contractor with a careless instruction. Loss from that breach of duty may occur when the instruction is carried out. The date when the claimant finds out about the instruction and the date when the consequences of that instruction become apparent are usually irrelevant when considering these sections. In order to mitigate the perceived hardship to claimants who may not find out about a breach of duty until long after the six years has elapsed, the Limitation Act 1980 provides at Section 14A a special provision which allows a claim to be taken in tort within three years of the date when the claimant had 'knowledge' of the matters giving rise to the claim, as defined by that section. Thus the claimant who discovers, seven years after the construction of his factory, that crucial fire dampers were omitted from the design, will be able to commence proceedings claiming a remedy in tort provided that he does so within three years of making the discovery.

Contributory negligence

The second special defence operates as a partial defence to a claim brought against a construction professional. The professional may be found to have been in breach of duty but may also be able to argue that the claimant was partially the author of his own misfortune by failing to take reasonable care to protect himself. For example a project manager engaged to carry out the construction of a factory may fail to warn his client that the special panels which the client wished to use were highly combustible and if employed in areas where there was a risk of fire would greatly increase the chance of fire spreading throughout the building. A fire may then take place which does indeed spread rapidly through the factory by reason of the presence of the panels. The claimant may seek to recover the entire loss caused by the fire. However, whilst the project manager may be partly to blame he may also succeed in making out a claim in contributory negligence against the claimant who did not take reasonable steps to prevent the outbreak of fire in the first place. As a result of this successful argument the court may reduce the damages which the project manager would have to pay by 50 per cent.[28]

28 See *Pride Valley Foods Ltd* v. *Hall & Partners (Contract Management) Ltd* [2001] 76 Con LR 1.

However, it should be noted that in order for such an argument to be successful the professional must be able to point to a lack of care on the part of the claimant which not only contributed to its loss but which was not concerned with the very risk which it was the professional's job to prevent. Thus in the foregoing example the project manager would not have been able to argue that the claimant was partially responsible for the loss because it should have known that the panels were highly flammable and should have done something about it. This was information which it was the project manager's job to provide. For this reason successful claims of contributory negligence are uncommon in claims made against construction professionals.

Apportionment and contribution

By contrast, it is very common for a construction professional against whom legal proceedings are taken to want to seek to apportion responsibility for the claimant's loss with another defendant or another person whom the professional believes was also responsible. Because of the complexity of modern building projects loss or damage suffered by an employer may often be the result of breaches of duty by a number of persons. These may all be professionals or they may be professionals and the contractor. Sometimes the employer will take legal proceedings against all such persons and sometimes he may only sue one or two of them, leaving those who have been sued to attempt to recover from the other persons also responsible. Where all the persons responsible for loss and damage are sued by a claimant, the court will usually decide which bears what element of responsibility and will 'apportion' damages between them. However, in most cases, and in particular where a professional seeks to blame a party not sued by the claimant, the professional will seek a contribution under the provisions of the Civil Liability (Contribution) Act 1978. This Act provides that a person who is liable to a claimant for loss or damage may recover a just and equitable contribution from another person who is liable for the same damage. Thus suppose that the employer finds that the flooring in the recently constructed warehouse has been defectively designed. He may sue the architect who was primarily responsible for the design. The architect may seek to join the structural engineer into the proceedings on the basis that his inadequate calculations were also a cause of the defective design and he should make a just and equitable contribution to whatever damages the architect is eventually ordered to pay. Frequently a claimant will complain that he has suffered different types of loss or damage as a result of a number of breaches of duty on the part of various professionals. In that situation the process of apportionment and contribution has to be carefully focused on the precise loss or damage concerned and the persons responsible for that loss or damage. Sometimes a claim made against a construction professional may be compromised before the claim for contribution made by that professional is litigated or even commenced. This is not a bar to those contribution proceedings taking place.

Whilst it is usual to resolve contribution issues at the same time as the other issues in the main action it is quite possible to claim a contribution after a settlement of the main action. Lastly, it should be noted that just as construction professionals may take contribution proceedings against other persons so these proceedings can be taken against construction professionals, either by another professional or, as sometimes happens, by the contractor.

2 Insurance

For all professionals engaged in the construction industry the obtaining of professional indemnity insurance is essential. Many of their professional bodies – for example the Architects' Registration Board – insist that they carry such insurance. Similarly, for most employers or contractors contemplating engaging the services of professionals engaged in construction related work, the availability of professional indemnity insurance is a paramount consideration. Often employers or contractors will insist upon the professional disclosing details of his professional indemnity cover and sometimes it is a requirement that specific cover is obtained for the project. If a dispute arises between an employer or contractor and the professional engaged by him the professional's defence will usually be conducted by solicitors appointed by his indemnity insurers, decisions as to whether to contest and at what level to settle the dispute will be taken by those insurers and the limit on recovery in the claim may well depend upon the limit of insurance carried by the professional under his indemnity policy. Consequently it is essential for both professionals and those employing them to be aware of the way in which indemnity policies work and the practical consequences which they entail for disputes involving construction professionals.

Professional indemnity policies

A professional indemnity policy is a policy of insurance taken out by a professional in order to protect him against liabilities incurred in carrying out his professional functions. A copy of the APIA–RIBA 2002 policy wording is annexed at Appendix 1. These policies commonly contain the following ingredients.

A description of the person benefiting from the policy

This will be the professional, sometimes identified by name but more usually identified by reference to his firm or the company which employs him. Typically he will be described as 'the insured'. In a firm 'the insured' will be usually defined as the partners of the firm (existing during the currency of the insurance), the former partners of the firm carrying out services for the firm, the estates or legal representatives of partners of the firm who were partners during the currency of the insurance but who have died or have become insolvent. The definition may go on to include other named persons (for example consultants).

The identity of the insurer

The insurer may be a number of persons who together subscribe to the policy of insurance. For most professional indemnity policies the Insurer is a company. However, it may be a list of companies or persons and in particular a list of Lloyds underwriters.

The nature of the risk insured

Usually the professional's insurance will cover 'civil liability' which arises from the insured's professional business. In most professional indemnity policies professional business will be defined quite broadly so as to include the work normally undertaken by that professional. Thus in an architect's policy it might be defined as services and/or advice commonly provided by members of the RIBA. An architect who is sued by his neighbour as a result of allegedly negligent advice concerning the development of the neighbour's property may therefore be entitled to claim an indemnity under the policy. An architect who is sued by his neighbour as a result of negligently backing his car into the neighbour's property will not. However, it is always open to an insured to seek to agree with the insurer that cover will be provided for other, more unusual services and these will be added to the policy by means of a schedule. Sometimes the policy will be limited geographically – for example it may apply only to professional business carried on in England and Wales.

The period of insurance

Professional indemnity policies provide cover for *claims made* during a particular period, being the period of insurance. For example an engineer's professional indemnity policy which provides indemnity cover for the year 2003–4 will indemnify the engineer against claims made against him in that period. The term 'claims made' is something of a term of art in insurance law (see the discussion below); however, it generally refers to the first notification of a claim against the professional. It is important to distinguish this point in time from (1) the date when the event occurred which gave rise to the claim – for example the giving of the allegedly negligent advice, (2) the date when the claim is first notified to the insurer and (3) the date when the professional admits the claim or a judgment is entered against him or he otherwise becomes 'liable.' All these dates are important, but the policy covers only 'claims made' – being claims first notified to the professional – during the period of its currency.

The limit of cover

Professional indemnity policies indemnify the professional against the prescribed liabilities. This means that the whole of a professional's liability to an employer or a contractor is paid by the insurer, subject to any 'excess' (for example the first £25,000) which is paid by the professional. Usually the Insurer is also obliged to pay all the employer's or contractor's legal costs and to meet the professional's legal costs. However, all policies are subject to a limit of liability, being the sum above which the insurer is not required to pay. Thus a project manager may carry professional indemnity insurance provided by insurer X in the sum of £10 million for any claim. In the event of his becoming vulnerable to a liability in the sum of £15 million he would be uninsured for the remaining £5 million. For this reason it is common for professionals to obtain 'top-up' insurance which covers them for their vulnerability above the primary level of cover. In our example the project manager might have obtained such cover in respect of the next slice of liability to the limit of a further £10 million from insurer Y. Some policies seek to apply the limit to the aggregate of all claims made during the relevant period. If the project manager in our example faced two claims in the relevant year, each giving rise to a liability of £10 million, he might find (depending on what other insurance he possessed) that he was covered only for the first claim in time and that he was without cover against the second. Clearly it is important for professionals and those contemplating employing them to be confident that the level of cover on any professional indemnity policy is appropriate to the level of risk.

Exclusions

All professional indemnity policies will provide a list of exclusions, being circumstances in which no indemnity will be provided. Some of these may seem obvious – for example such policies commonly exclude liability arising out of disputes with employees and losses arising out of injury, illness, injury or death caused to the insured or their employees, risks arising from nuclear accidents or wars. Others merely affirm what is said elsewhere – for example excluding cover for that much of the liability as constitutes the excess. However, other exclusions are both important and potentially problematic. Most policies will exclude claims arising out of fraud or dishonesty on the part of the insured or other persons. However, the extent to which that loss is excluded and the circumstances in which it will be wholly or partially excluded vary from policy to policy. (This is to be contrasted with fraud or dishonesty in the obtaining of insurance and/or pursuing of a claim which almost always leads to a loss of cover – see below.) Similarly most policies will exclude – in whole or in part – losses arising on commercial ventures where the professional is a joint participant (thus avoiding the risk that the professional will share in the proceeds of the policy). An important exclusion concerns claims which might fall under other policies of insurance. It is quite possible that a claim will be made in such circumstances that it might be covered under two or more different policies held by the insured. Insurers try to protect their policy from having to pay out in such circumstances by insisting that the professional look to the other policy or policies first. However, because the other policy or policies will often contain similar exclusions the effect is generally that they cancel each other out and the insurers decide amongst themselves who will bear what share of the liability.

General conditions

All professional indemnity policies contain general conditions with which the professional is required to comply. In some policies these conditions are expressed to be 'conditions precedent' to the provision of indemnity. This generally means that failure to comply will entitle the insurer to decline indemnity even though the failure may be a technical one and/or may have caused the Insurer no real harm. However, most policies for construction professionals are more benign and there are few if any conditions precedent, instead the gravity of any breach of condition will be assessed in deciding whether the insurer is entitled to decline indemnity. That is not to say that even benign policies cannot require strict compliance. Most if not all policies will have an express requirement that the insured do not make or pursue any fraudulent claim and if fraud is employed there will be no obligation to indemnify (even if the fraud was small and affected only part of an otherwise good claim). Other important conditions which can be applied strictly, albeit not as strictly as in the case of fraud, are the obligation to notify the insurer promptly of circumstances which may give rise to a claim (see discussion below) and the obligation not to prejudice the insurer's position in respect of any legal proceedings (also discussed below). Other standard general conditions concern the professional's obligation to assist the Insurer, which usually extends to permitting the insurer to sue third parties in the name of the professional to recover sums paid out by the insurer and provisions dealing with the applicable law (i.e. English law) and the means for dealing with certain disputes between the professional and the Insurer.

Obtaining cover

Cover under a professional indemnity policy is normally obtained though an intermediary known as an insurance broker or by contacting an insurer direct.[1] The advantage of using a broker is that he will be retained by the

---

1 Professional bodies such as the RIBA promote recommended schemes or recommend particular brokers.

professional in order to obtain the most suitable insurance policy, having had regard to the professional's circumstances, the nature of the risk and the costs of available policies. He will also guide an inexperienced professional through the various parts of the proposal, ensuring that the professional understands the nature of the document and his obligations to provide information. As brokers obtain their commission from the insurer and do not generally charge the professional for their services it is usually both cost-effective and commercially advisable to place professional indemnity insurance through a broker. Certainly where professionals require complex cover – for example cover in relation to one particular project or cover over and above a standard indemnity limit – it is almost always sensible to seek it though a broker. Moreover the services of a broker are usually required where the professional requires immediate cover. Here a broker can usually arrange interim cover which will protect the professional until the insurer has had time to consider his proposal or application. In some instances brokers have authority from insurers to authorise this cover themselves.

The insurance broker, or alternatively the insurer, will provide the professional with the proposal form, which is usually in a standard form generated by the insurer. The professional's proposal for the provision of professional indemnity cover will form the basis of the professional's contract with the insurer and to that end it seeks all the information which the insurer believes it needs to know in order to assess the risk and decide whether or not to accept the insurance. For this reason the forms will frequently ask questions concerning the size and nature of the professional's business, the types of work commonly undertaken by him and likely to be undertaken during the likely period of cover, whether the professional has been refused cover by any other insurer and so forth. The form will usually provide space for the professional to inform the prospective insurer of any other facts or matters which the insurer ought to know about. This curious provision is a special feature of all contracts of insurance and concerns what is commonly referred to as the insured's *duty of utmost good faith*. As with any contract, an insurance policy can be ineffective if it was procured by fraud or misrepresentation. However, contracts of insurance are distinguished by imposing on the person seeking insurance a duty of utmost good faith: the proposer is obliged to disclose to the insurer at the time of making (or remaking) the contract of insurance all material information affecting the risk. Thus, for example, a proposal form may ask the architect general questions about his work, his claims record and so forth, all of which the architect answers truthfully. However, the architect may be aware of a particular risk which would not be apparent to the insurer from that information (for example that the partner currently running a very high-risk project was on the point of leaving the firm). The obligation of utmost good faith probably requires the architect to disclose that information to the insurer. The obligation arises because:

Insurance is a contract of speculation. The special facts upon which the contingent chance is to be computed lie most commonly in the knowledge of the insured only; the underwriter trusts to his representation, and proceeds upon the confidence that he does not keep back any circumstance.[2]

It will be noted that the important consideration is that the information must be *material* to a consideration of the risk. The materiality of information is a question of fact, determined by reference to the judgment of the reasonable insurer at the time that the proposer is obliged to disclose. The 'reasonable insurer' is of course just as much a legal construct as the 'reasonably careful professional' and when disputes concerning these issues come to court the court will hear evidence from expert witnesses as to what the response would have been to any particular fact from a 'reasonable insurer'. Materiality in this context means that it would be taken into account by the reasonable insurer in deciding whether and on what terms to offer insurance. Indeed if an insurer later seeks to rely on non-disclosure in order to make the policy ineffectual (to 'avoid' the policy) he must establish not merely that the information was material but that it actually would have led to a different result had it been communicated to him.[3] Moreover the proposer is required not merely to disclose material facts of which he has actual knowledge, but material facts which he ought to know – at least in so far as it is a circumstance which in the ordinary course of business he ought to know. An indication as to the kinds of matters which the insurer is likely to regard as being material will be provided by the questions on the policy. Similarly the questions may indicate the extent to which information is likely to be regarded as immaterial. If the insurer requests the claims record of an engineer for the last five years it is a fair inference that he regards the claims record more than five years previously as irrelevant. It is the duty of the broker to take reasonable steps to ensure that a proposer understands his obligations of disclosure, and often a broker will ask supplementary questions to this end.

Most professional indemnity policies fall to be renewed on an annual basis. If a broker is acting for the professional he will be under an obligation to take reasonable steps to ensure that the professional is aware in good time that his policy is due for renewal, and most insurers liaising directly with professionals will be in contact well before the renewal date. Renewal generally does not require a fresh proposal, but is usually effected by communication between the broker, acting on the professional's instructions, and the insurer. Although technically a fresh contract, the professional is entitled to expect all the previous terms to remain the same unless his broker has

---

2 *Carter* v. *Boehm* (1766) 3 Burr 1905 at 1909 per Lord Mansfield.
3 *Pan Atlantic Insurance Co.* v. *Pine Top Insurance Co.* [1995] AC 501.

been notified to the contrary by the insurer. In practice, apart from changes in the premium, there may be minor variations in some of the clauses or the professional may require slightly different cover and to update schedules to the policy dealing with the constitution of the firm, the names of consultants and so forth. However, it is important to note that, as with any fresh contract of insurance, the professional is again under a duty of utmost good faith which requires him to inform the insurer (usually through the broker) of facts and matters which ought to be brought to the Insurer's attention.

The cost of professional indemnity insurance, the *premium*, may be payable in one tranche or in stages depending upon the terms of the policy. Most policies will contain express terms that stipulate that cover lapses (or even does not commence) in the event of the professional's failure to provide the premium on time.

Claims made and indemnity

Most professional indemnity policies operate on a *claims made* basis. Typically they will have wording along these lines:

> 3.1 The Assured is indemnified against any claim made during the Period of Insurance for which the Assured shall become legally liable to pay compensation together with claimant's costs, fees and expenses in accordance with any judgment, award or settlement made within the Geographical Limits in consequence of:
>
> 3.1.1 Any breach of the professional duty of care owed by the Assured to the claimant which term is deemed to include a breach of warranty of authority;
>
> 3.1.2 Any libel, slander or slander of title, slander of goods or injurious falsehood;
>
> 3.1.3 The loss, destruction of or damage to any document in the care, custody and control of the Assured or for which the Assured is responsible (except to the extent insured by Section 4);
>
> 3.1.4 Any unintentional breach of copyright by the Assured or any employee of the Assured.[4]

As stated above, the operative moment in time is therefore not the time of the event which gives rise to the breach of duty or the time when the professional becomes under a liability in respect of the breach of duty but rather the moment when the employer or contractor indicates to the professional that he is contemplating making a claim against him. In *Robert Irving &*

---

4 APIA–RIBA 2002 Wording.

Burns v. *Stone*[5] Staughton LJ restated the commonly accepted view that 'in the ordinary meaning of the English language the words "claims made" indicate that there has been a communication by the client to the [Insured] surveyor of some discontent which will, or may, result in a remedy expected from the surveyor. There must be communication.' What in practice constitutes intimation of a claim? There is little difficulty over solicitors' letters stating that a claim is to be pursued in court, nor is there any obvious difficulty about the service of legal proceedings. However, what of communications which fall short of this level of immediate threat? For example, on a difficult job the employer may complain to the architect at regular intervals that he is not happy with this or that aspect of progress or the development of the design or that he is concerned that in some way the architect is not doing his job properly. Such communication may go so far as to state that the employer will hold the architect responsible for this or that anticipated loss. At what point will these letters develop into the intimation of a claim? The practical answer is that provided that the various events which might constitute intimation of a claim fall within a period of insurance it is unlikely to matter greatly what precise moment in time is chosen. There may be differences in the excess for different years and occasionally relevant terms of the policy may be different. However, in the generality of cases, providing there has been adequate notification (see below), no practical problems arise.

However, there are three instances where it may be of crucial importance to professionals as to when a claim is made. The first is concerned with professionals who are on the point of retiring or changing their business and who may require 'run-off' insurance to cover the risk that claims will be made many years after the alleged breaches of duty which gave rise to them. In such situations there is often a risk that the run-off cover may not be adequate to indemnify against very late claims made and a professional seeking such cover should always explore with the broker the way in which any run-off cover will respond to such claims. The second potential area of difficulty concerns situations where a professional changes his insurer. Here there is the risk that although he may know of the possibility that a claim will be intimated against him, such intimation is unlikely to take place in the remaining period of cover with the existing insurer. Were he now to seek insurance from a new insurer in respect of the period during which a claim would be likely to be made, the new insurer would be entitled to be informed about the circumstances which might give rise to the claim to be made and might refuse to provide insurance altogether, or might provide it only at a greatly enhanced premium or most likely might seek to exclude that particular set of circumstances from the accepted risks. (The existing insurer would probably be deprived of this option by the terms of his existing policy.)

5 [1998] Lloyds Rep IR 258.

It is for this reason that professionals are well advised not to change their insurers too frequently. Thirdly, if a number of claims of significant value are made in any one year, the total value of the claims may be aggregated with the result that the available cover is exhausted. In this eventuality the later made claim or claims may fall partially or wholly outside the cover provided by the policy.

There is a further problem concerning the formulation of claims made which is of concern to professionals in the construction industry. An action or an omission to act by a construction professional may have a number of consequences. Furthermore one or more matters which arise as a result of a construction professional's conduct may arise because of a series of acts and/or failures to act. If all the problems which flow from one action or omission are reported separately and at different times, does that amount to one claim or a number of claims? Alternatively if a number of actions or omissions give rise to a range of consequences which are complained of together does that amount to one claim? The answer may be important in two ways. First, depending on the precise wording of the policy – and in particular whether there is any sort of aggregation clause – there is a risk to the insured that the totting up of a number of different 'losses' will lead to a liability in excess of the indemnity limit and very possibly in excess of the total cover carried by the insured. Clearly in such situations it may be in the insured's interests to contend that these are all separate claims, each of which falls to be dealt with singly, whilst the insurer may be tempted to treat them all as one claim, disclaiming any indemnity over the indemnity limit. Secondly there is the converse position concerning excess. Under most professional indemnity policies the insured will pay an excess in respect of each claim. Clearly in a situation where there are a large number of small claims the insured may end up paying the lion's share of the liability because the policy will respond only to a modest element in each claim. Here it may be in the insured's interests to contend for one claim whilst the insurer will want to argue that this is a case of separate small claims.

In *Thorman and others* v. *New Hampshire Insurance Co. and others*[6] the architects had changed insurer, transferring to the new insurer after notification to the old one of the possibility of a claim and after the issue of proceedings but before receiving service of those proceedings or any (substantive) letter of claim. After the transfer the claim against the architects was duly served and consisted of a wide number of disparate complaints, some of which had been notified to the first insurer, but some of which had not. The two insurers each refused indemnity, arguing that the other was responsible and, in the case of the second insurer, that it was entitled to avoid the policy because of the architects' failure to disclose the facts of the circumstances giving rise to the claim. The Court of Appeal decided that the first

6 [1988] 1 Lloyds Rep 7.

insurers were entirely liable on the basis that although a claim might not have been made prior to the period of transfer, because the claim had been notified and because of the special wording of the policy the first insurer was not entitled to argue that the claim was not made until after it had ceased cover. Moreover on the facts of this case all the allegations amounted to one single claim; however, in so doing the court had to consider the general approach to be taken to the issue of whether there were a number of different claims or one claim. The court decided that in each case the answer was a question of fact to be decided on the basis of the circumstances of each case. However, Donaldson MR provided some useful guidelines:

> Let me take some examples. An architect has separate contracts with separate building owners. The architect makes the same negligent mistake in relation to each. The claims have a factor in common, namely the same negligent mistake, and to this extent are related, but clearly they are separate claims. Bringing the claims a little closer together, let us suppose that the architect has a single contract in relation to two separate houses to be built on quite separate sites in different parts of the country. If one claim is in respect of a failure to specify windows of the requisite quality and the other is in respect of a failure to supervise the laying of foundations, I think that once again the claims would be separate. But it would be otherwise if the complaint was the same in relation to both houses. The take the present example of a single contract for professional services in relation to a number of houses in a single development. A single complaint that they suffered from a wide range of unrelated defects and a demand for compensation would, I think, be regarded as a single claim. But if the defences manifested themselves seriatim and each gave rise to a separate complaint, what then? They might be regarded as separate claims. Alternatively later complaints could be regarded as enlargement of the original claims that the architect had been professionally negligent in his execution of his contract. It would, I think, very much depend upon the facts.

Notification

All policies of professional indemnity insurance require the professional to give prompt notification of claims made against them. Moreover, depending on the precise wording of the policy, they are usually required to give notification of circumstances which *may* give rise to a claim. Thus, for example, the APIA–RIBA 2002 wording provides that:

Notification Procedures

6.2 The Assured shall as a condition precedent to their right to be indemnified under:

    6.2.1 Section 3 of this Policy, give notice in writing to Insurers as soon as possible during the Period of Insurance of any claim or of the receipt of notice from any person of an intention to make a claim and regardless of any previous notice, give notice in writing immediately on receipt of any Claim Form, Particulars of Claim, Arbitration Notice or any other formal document commencing legal proceedings of any kind.

    6.2.2 Section 4.1 of this Policy, give notice in writing to Insurers as soon as possible during the Period of Insurance if during such Period of Insurance they shall discover that any document has been destroyed or damaged or lost or mislaid.

6.3 The Assured shall give during the Period of Insurance full details in writing as soon as possible of any circumstance or event of which the Assured shall first become aware during the Period of Insurance. Any such circumstance or event notified to Insurers during the Period of Insurance which subsequently gives rise to a claim shall be deemed to be a claim made during the Period of Insurance.

6.4 Receipt by the Assured of any 'Notice of Adjudication' and/or a 'referral notice' pursuant to the Scheme for Construction Contracts Regulations 1997 under the Housing Grants, Construction and Regeneration Act 1996 and/or any adjudication notice pursuant to contract must be notified immediately in writing to Fishburn's, Solicitors, 61 St Mary Axe, London EC3A 8AA.

6.5 Notification of a 'notice of adjudication' and/or 'referral notice' and/or any adjudication notice pursuant to contract to Fishburn's Morgan Cole in writing will be considered as notification to Insurers. All other circumstances, claims and material facts must be notified to Insurers as per policy terms, conditions, limitations and exclusions.

6.6 It is agreed that Insurers shall be entitled to pursue legal, arbitration or other proceedings in the name of and on behalf of the Assured to challenge, appeal, open up or amend any decision, direction, award, or the exercise of any power of the Adjudicator or to stay the enforcement of any decision, direction, award or exercise of any power of the Adjudicator. The Assured shall give all such assistance as Insurers may reasonably require in relation to such proceedings. For the avoidance of doubt this section does not in any way limit Insurers' rights to subrogation.

6.7 Notice to Insurers to be given under this Policy shall be deemed to be properly made if received in writing by RIBA Insurance Agency Limited., at the address shown in the Schedule.

6.8 For the avoidance of doubt notice hereunder can *only* be made by the Assured (or agent of the Assured) and *not* by any other party).

The purpose of such clauses is to enable the insurer to take prompt steps to investigate the circumstances of the claim before the trail of surrounding evidence goes cold. Furthermore in certain circumstances it may enable the Insurer to take active steps in preparation for a claim such as the obtaining of reports. It will be noted that because of this requirement such clauses always contain a statement that the date of notification will count as the date when the claim was made (if one is subsequently made). This is for the obvious reason that the claim may not be made for quite some time and if it were not for this kind of provision it would be open to the insurer to withdraw cover or raise the premiums to take account of the new risk.

Prompt notification of claims is a matter of considerable importance to insurers and often professional indemnity policies will make such prompt notification a condition precedent of indemnity. Consequently it is important for a construction professional to be aware of the nature of the obligation imposed by these clauses. Generally speaking indemnity policies fall into two camps as to the way in which the duty to report is couched. The more generous policies require the professional to report circumstances which are *likely* to give rise to a claim. This imposes a test of 'at least 50 per cent probability of giving rise to a claim' judged, objectively, at the time when the fact or matter comes to the attention of the professional.[7] Thus where the professional is aware that actions or omissions on his part give rise to a possibility that the client, rightly or wrongly, may make a claim against him in the future, he must go on an take an objective view of that likelihood. If it seems to him more likely than not that the events will give rise to a claim he should notify his insurers immediately. By contrast many professional indemnity policies employ a much lower threshold by requiring the professional to report circumstances which *may* to give rise to a claim. The standard here is harder to judge and all that can be safely said about it is that it imposes a lower than 50 per cent threshold. At various times different phrases have been used to provide guidance as to the obligation – it arises if the insured 'ought to have contemplated that it was an occurrence which *might* result in a claim for compensation',[8] alternatively it arises when there are circumstances which 'may give rise to a claim,' when a claim was 'at least possible'[9] – however, it appears that the best approach is to provide notification in

7 *Layher* v. *Lowe* [2000] 1 Lloyds Rep IR 510.
8 *General Motors* v. *Crowder* (1931) 40 Ll L Rep 87.
9 *Rothschild* v. *Collyer* [1999] Lloyds Rep IR 6.

any circumstances where the professional recognises that there is a *realistic possibility* that a claim will result. It should be noted that, in either case, when assessing whether a professional has complied with his duty to notify it is unlikely to be a defence that the insured was too busy or took the view that he ought to wait and see how things developed before giving notification. Moreover a court would be likely to find that the obligation in either case arises not just in respect of matters which the professional actually knew but matters which he ought reasonably to have known – thus it will be no excuse that the professional buried his head in the sand and was thus oblivious to the problems which later gave rise to a claim.[10] Of course the professional is unlikely to have imputed to him knowledge of a design defect arising at the moment when the design was produced – that would undermine the whole point of obtaining the insurance, which was, in part, to safeguard the professional from the financial consequences of his own negligence – however, once the consequences of the defective design begin to manifest themselves the professional will be expected to be reasonably astute as to their possible causes and if one of these is his own defaults, notification should follow.

What is prompt notification – for example 'notification as soon as possible' – is a question of fact in each case. Where an event takes place that is clear and is obviously likely to lead to a claim, notification should be made within a matter of days. However, where the problem emerges gradually, is complicated and where the judgment as to whether it may or is likely to give rise to a claim is more difficult, the professional will generally be provided with greater latitude. Indeed it is not unknown for claims to be intimated before notification takes place because the professional was, justifiably, gathering material upon which to take a view as to whether or not to notify. In practice the golden rule is to play safe and if in doubt provide notification. As notification is generally made to the insurance broker this can be as informal as a telephone conversation, although it will usually be confirmed in writing. As the agent of the insured the insurer is deemed to have received such notification even if the broker fails to communicate it or misdescribes what he has been told.

Handling of claims

As stated above, the insurer will usually require prompt notification of the risk of claims so that he can take steps to investigate and prepare for the defence of any claim. However, in many, if not the majority of, cases the insurer will take no action at this stage other than (perhaps) to require that further information be provided and to require that the professional keep it informed as to developments. Indeed even after a claim is intimated,

---

10 See *Layher* v. *Lowe* (1996) 58 Con LR 42.

for example by a solicitors' letter, the insurer *may* decide to take no further steps at that point, leaving the professional to deal with the situation as best he can. In practice, however, once a solicitor's letter threatening a claim on behalf of an employer or a contractor has been delivered to a professional he will forward this document to the insurer who will then take over all contact on the matter with the employer or contractor, often through one of the firms of solicitors on the insurer's panel of solicitors. The insured is unlikely to have much if any say in the selection of this firm, although generally speaking they are likely to be highly experienced in dealing with negligence claims against professionals. As a rule the insurer will undertake the defence and will be obliged to bear the costs of that defence. Whilst the solicitors are retained jointly by the professional and the Insurer, their primary client will remain the insurer but *only* in so far as the terms of the policy require the professional to concede to the insurer. Otherwise solicitors acting for the professional and the insurer are not permitted to prefer the interests of one client over the other, and in the event of a conflict of interest arising they must so inform both their clients and may well be prevented from continuing to act further.

In the majority of cases there is no disagreement or conflict of interest between the professional and his Insurer. However, conflicts and similar problems can arise and it is important for the professional to be aware of them. The most important type of problem which can arise is that the insurer can decide not to provide an indemnity because, it alleges, the professional has failed to comply with one of the conditions precedent in the contract of insurance. Commonly this happens because, having investigated the background, the insurer takes the view that the professional failed to provide prompt notification of the possibility of a claim (although in practice indemnity is rarely declined unless the insurer has suffered some real prejudice as a result), but other circumstances include:

1 The cover provided for in the contract of insurance does not apply to the claim made against the professional. For example the claim may relate to the activities of a consultant who is not included under the definition of the insured, or the activity may be outside the usual scope of that professional's business. Many policies exclude claims arising out of the fraudulent or criminal conduct of the professional (but see below).

2 The professional may have made admissions or taken other steps which prejudice the insurer's prospects of defending the claim. All professional indemnity policies require professionals to take no action which might provide an admission or compromise part of a claim and which will make it harder for the insurer to defend any legal proceedings. Where the insurer has suffered real harm as a result of a breach of this obligation by a professional it may, depending on the wording of the policy, decline to provide an indemnity. (It is for this reason that no matter how well a professional gets on with his employer, and no matter how reasonable

he wishes to appear, he should generally never make an admission that he acted in breach of duty.)

3   In the formulation of his proposal or in obtaining a renewal of insurance the professional failed to inform the insurer of a matter which should have been passed on to him in compliance with the professional's duty of utmost good faith. In these circumstances the entire policy may be avoided – i.e. treated as never having existed.

4   The professional may have employed some fraudulent means in the pursuit of the claim – he may have deliberately concealed the true nature of the events or the fact that he had a secret financial interest in the insurance proceeds. In such cases the insurer will usually avoid the policy.

It should be noted that one of the advantages of obtaining cover under a policy wording provided by or recommended by the RIBA, RICS or other similar professional body is that quite often the wording is unusually favourable to the professional in respect of the circumstances where cover will be declined. For example Condition 7 of the APIA–RIBA 2002 wording states:

7.1   Insurers will not exercise their right to avoid the Policy nor will Insurers reject a request for indemnity when it is alleged that there has been:

7.1.1   Non-disclosure of facts; or
7.1.2   Misrepresentation of facts; or
7.1.3   Incorrect particulars or statements; or
7.1.4   Late notification of a claim; or
7.1.5   Late notification of intention to make a claim; or
7.1.6   Late notification of a circumstance or event.

7.2   Provided this condition shall not apply to any claim known to the Assured prior to inception of this Policy.

7.3   Provided also that the Assured shall establish to Insurers' satisfaction that such alleged non-disclosure, misrepresentation or incorrect particulars or statements or late notice was innocent and free of any fraudulent conduct or intent to deceive.

7.4   When Insurers are so satisfied the following conditions shall apply:

7.4.1   Nothing in this clause shall entitle the Assured to indemnity wider or more extensive than is available to the Assured under this Policy (notwithstanding the terms of this clause).

7.4.2   Where the Assured's conduct or breach of or non-compliance with any condition of this Policy has resulted in prejudice to the handling or settlement of any claim, the indemnity afforded by this Policy in respect of such claim (including defence costs) shall be reduced to such sum as in Insurers' opinion would have been payable by them in the absence of such prejudice.

7.4.3 No indemnity shall be available for any claim, intention to make a claim, circumstance or event notified to Insurers after the Period of Insurance.

7.5 In the event of any disagreement by the Assured regarding the application of these Special Conditions, such disagreement shall at the Assured's request be referred to the person nominated by the President for the time being of the Royal Institute of British Architects for his consideration and intercession on the Assured's behalf if the facts are considered to warrant this by the person so nominated, and the Insurers agree to give due and proper consideration to any such intercession.

Disputes as to cover generally arise early, sometimes even before a claim is intimated. This is not only because one of the first concerns to the insurer is whether indemnity should be provided at all, but also because the longer the insurer acts for the insured in any proceedings and/or gives the impression that cover is being provided the more likely it is that it will be prevented from declining cover on the basis that it has waived its right to do so or that it is estopped from doing so. A *waiver* occurs where an insurer knowingly acts in such a way as to confirm, in the eyes of the law, that it is giving up its entitlement to take a stand upon a certain point. An *estoppel* acts similarly where the law finds that it would be inequitable for an insurer to take advantage of a point when his previous conduct had suggested that he would not and the professional relied upon that suggestion. Typically an insurer may continue to conduct the defence of a claim against a professional although both the insurer and the professional know that the insurer has information which would entitle him to avoid the policy. The professional may thus be led to believe that the insurer will not seek to take advantage of that information and should the insurer later seek to do so that action may be held invalid. Although insurers will usually seek to protect themselves by stating that they are acting 'without prejudice' to their rights under the policy the longer the matter continues and the more firmly the insurer creates the impression that he has decided not to decline cover the more likely it is that a waiver or estoppel will be established. Where a dispute as to cover emerges the professional should immediately retain his own solicitors. He will require advice as to the dispute itself – and in particular what to do about it – and as to the defence of the claim made against him. As stated above, the solicitors originally instructed by the insurer on behalf of both the professional and the Insurer are unlikely to be able to continue acting.

What happens if there is a disagreement between the professional and the insurer over whether to contest the claim? Often, particularly if the excess is modest compared with the inconvenience and adverse publicity which might flow from contesting a claim (not to mention the damage to commercial relationships with important clients), professionals are reluctant to contest certain claims which the insurer believes ought to be contested on their merits. Similarly in a situation where the potential claim will be in excess of the level of indemnity the professional is often keen to try to settle at a figure within the indemnity cover so as to avoid the risk that he will be exposed to an element of the compensation under the claim which falls outside the indemnity. In contrast the insurer may take the view that there is much to be said for contesting the proceedings. Under some policies the insurer is given the final say. However, many policies contain a 'QC' clause along the following lines:

> [The insurer will pay] any such claim or claims which may arise without requiring the assured to dispute any claim, unless a Queen's Counsel (to be mutually agreed upon by the underwriters and assured) advise that the same could be successfully contested by the assured and the assured consents to such a claim being contested, but such consent not to be unreasonably withheld.[11]

On occasion the insurer wishes not to contest the claim and it is the professional who wants it to be fought, and often the clause will provide for both the insurer and the insured to refer the claim to the QC in this way. If not, the insurer usually reserves the right to compromise claims.

A further potential source of disagreement between the professional and the insurer concerns the professional's claim for fees. It is usually the case that a construction professional who is sued by the employer or contractor will be owed fees which the employer or contractor has refused to pay. In such circumstances it is quite common for the professional to counterclaim for his fees. Conversely very often professional negligence actions against construction professionals arise after the professional has sought payment of the remainder of his fees and has commenced proceedings to obtain that payment. The employer or contractor then counterclaims, alleging professional negligence. Professional indemnity policies do not purport to indemnify the professional for the loss of his fees, nor do they usually provide that the defence costs (which are paid by the insurer) will extend to covering the pursuit of the professional's fees. By the same token, the extent of the indemnity provided by the insurer is not reduced to take into account the corresponding benefit of fees owed to the professional and the insurer cannot, without the professional's agreement, settle an action on the basis that the professional will forgo his fees.

---

11 Taken from *West Wake Price & Co. v. Ching* [1957] 1 WLR 45.

Subrogation

Many professional indemnity policies will contain a reference to the insurer's right of *subrogation*. The right of subrogation is the insurer's right to take steps to seek compensation from other persons, as if he was the insured professional, corresponding to insurance payments he has made on behalf of the insured. Typically an insurer might settle a claim brought by an employer in respect of defective work undertaken by an engineer. The defective work might have been that of a consultant subcontracted to the engineer. The insurer would sue the consultant in the name of the engineer to recover the monies paid out. The right of subrogation operates as a matter of law and does not require any provision in the policy. However, professional indemnity policies frequently contain a provision whereby the insurer agrees not to exercise his right of subrogation against the employees of the professional unless there has been fraud or some similar conduct on the part of the employee.

Insurance and persons claiming against professionals

For employers or contractors wishing to claim against professionals the existence of and extent of professional indemnity cover will be a crucial consideration. Many employers, particularly local authority employers, insist upon full disclosure of the professional indemnity cover as a precondition of engagement. However, where this has not happened it can generally be assumed that most reputable construction professionals will carry some professional indemnity cover, although that does not mean that in any particular case the limit of indemnity has not already been exhausted by other claims in the relevant period or that the cover will not be avoided for reasons of non-disclosure or otherwise. Furthermore the employer or contractor is unlikely to know the extent of cover, which may be a significant matter in a larger claim. It is usual for letters of claim against construction professionals to contain the request that the professional's insurers be notified and even to request details of who the Insurers are.

However, the person making a claim against a construction professional generally has no direct right of action against that professional's insurer and there is little he can do to affect a dispute between that professional and his insurer over the level of indemnity. In *Normid Housing Association Ltd* v. *Ralphs & Mansell and others*[12] (see below) the claimant housing association brought a claim against a firm of architects. The architect was in dispute with his insurers about the extent to which his policy provided indemnity against the claims made by the association. The housing association learned that the architect and the insurers were ready to come to an agreement whereby

12 (1990) 21 Con LR 98.

the scope of cover would be applied narrowly so that some of the association's claims would fall outside the indemnity. Accordingly the association sought an injunction preventing any agreement asserting that any such agreement was based on a misinterpretation of the policy and that its right to make recovery would be prejudiced by the agreement. The architect had not been under any contractual duty to obtain a particular level of insurance for the works and the Court of Appeal declined to grant the injunction. Slade LJ said of the architects:[13]

> The policies were their own assets and they were free to deal with their rights under them as with any others of their assets. They owed no professional duty of skill and care to the plaintiffs to deal or not deal with them in any particular way. Any such dealing would be right outside the course of their professional activities.

This example illustrates one of the important reasons why employers and contractors may wish to make the obtaining of adequate insurance, together with safeguards as to entitlement to the proceeds,[14] a term of engagement in relation to specific high value projects.

A measure of protection has been introduced for persons seeking to recover damages from professionals who, although insured, become insolvent prior to any liability being established against them. Prior to 1930 if a professional who had a liability to an employer became bankrupt at any stage prior to recovery of compensation from the professional's insurer the employer would have to prove in the bankruptcy for his entitlement and would rank behind the secured creditors. This situation brought about the Third Parties (Rights against Insurers) Act 1930 which sought to protect persons in the situation of the employer by removing the rights under the insurance policy from the insolvency process and transferring them directly to the third party. However, the courts have so interpreted the Act that there is no liability unless and until the employer has shown that the professional is liable for a particular loss. Thus if the professional has admitted the claim or has had judgment or an award made against him the Act will operate so as to enable the employer to seek payment from the insurer. But if there is no such proof of liability the employer will have to prove, and this may be difficult to do short of a full (and expensive) trial. It was for this reason that the Act was of no assistance to the housing association in *Normid*. There had been no admission of liability and no judgment and accordingly the association could not invoke its direct claim against the insurer. Further it should be noted that because the Act operates to vest the professional's rights against the insurer in the employer, it is still

---

13 At p. 110.
14 This would be done by means of a loss payable clause making the employer the beneficiary under the insurance contract and enabling him to enforce its terms by operation of the Contract (Rights of Third Parties) Act 1999.

open to the insurer to decline indemnity or the full scope of indemnity on any basis that it could have maintained against the professional.

Other insurance

There has been an increasing tendency over the last twenty years for employers and contractors on large projects to agree *project cover* – being insurance cover whereby the insurer underwrites the risk of defects arising in a period of ten years no matter how they arise. The advantage of such cover – often termed *decennial insurance* because it lasts for ten years – is that the employer and the contractor do not have to engage time and resources disagreeing over the presence of and responsibility for defects. The disadvantage is cost, such policies normally being priced at a percentage of the project sum. Much more common – indeed almost universal – is the obtaining by contractors of *contractors' all-risks insurance*, which contractors are required to obtain under many standard forms of building contract. These policies underwrite the risk of loss or damage to the works by reason of the negligence of the contractor.

Construction professionals need to take particular care when becoming involved in projects where such policies are in operation because of the risk that the insurers will look to them for the costs of paying out on the policy. This risk is illustrated by the case of *Co-operative Retail Services Ltd* v. *Taylor Young Partnership*.[15] CRS commissioned Wimpey to build an office block. TYP and another defendant, HLP, were engaged as architects and consulting engineers respectively. Under Wimpey's contract with CRS Wimpey was obliged to and did obtain contractors' all-risks insurance, to which the main electrical subcontractor, Hall, was also a party. A fire broke out and destroyed the office block. The insurers paid CRS substantial compensation for the costs of reinstatement and associated professional fees. Exercising their right of subrogation, they pursued TYP and HLP in the name of CRS, alleging that these professionals were at least partly to blame for the fire. TYP and CRS alleged that most if not all of the responsibility lay with Wimpey and Hall. They sought to claim contribution from Wimpey and Hall. However, the House of Lords held that because Wimpey and Hall were covered by the same insurance policy as gave rise to the subrogation they were not liable to CRS for any damage (even if in fact they had been to blame for the fire) and consequently no right of contribution lay against them. Counsel for TYP and HLP complained that this would be a very unjust result: they bore the entire financial liability for a catastrophe for which they may have had a very minor responsibility. However, the House of Lords held that the answer was that professionals in their position should have foreseen this risk and taken steps to avoid it, for example seeking to be included in the policy or negotiating contractual protections.

15 [2002] 1 WLR 1419.

3 Architects and engineers

Architects and engineers are taken together because of the common feature of design and the supervision of building to a design. To some extent the analysis in this chapter applies equally to any professional in the construction industry carrying out these functions, albeit that they are usually carried out by these two professions.

'Architect' and 'engineer'

The courts have traditionally defined an architect as a person possessing certain skills with regard to the design and supervision of building works.[1] The most satisfactory explanation of what an architect does is by reference to the duties he is commonly called upon to perform. These are recorded in Hudson as follows:

1   To advise and consult the employer (not as a lawyer) as to any limitation which may exist as to the use of the land to be built on, either (*inter alia*) by restrictive covenants or by the rights of adjoining owners or the public over the land, or by statutes and by-laws affecting the works to be executed.
2   To examine the site, subsoil and surroundings.
3   To consult and advise the employer as to the proposed work.
4   To prepare sketch plans and a specification, having regard to all the conditions which exist, and to submit them to the employer for approval with an estimate of the probable cost, if requested.
5   To elaborate and, if necessary, modify or amend the sketch plans as he may be instructed and prepare working drawings and a specification or specifications.
6   To consult and advise the employer as to obtaining tenders, whether by invitation or by advertisement, and as to the necessity or otherwise of employing a quantity surveyor.

---

1 See *R* v. *Architects' Registration Tribunal* ex parte *Jaggar* [1945] 2 AER 131 at 134.

7   To supply the builder with copies of the contract drawings and specification, supply such further drawings and give such instructions as may be necessary, supervise the work, and see that the contractor performs the contract, and advise the employer if he commits any serious breach thereof.

8   To perform his duties to his employer as defined by any contract with his employer or by the contract with the builder, and generally to act as the employer's agent in all matters connected with the work and the contract, except where otherwise prescribed by the contract with the builder, as, for instance, in cases where he has under the contract to act as arbitrator or quasi-arbitrator.

In the United Kingdom, in order to trade as an 'architect' a person must be registered by the Architects' Registration Board[2] which requires the applicant to have passed a recognised examination and to have certain practical experience. 'Trading'[3] means holding out architectural services as a material part of a business and trading as an architect when not registered is a criminal offence. Usually practising architects also belong to the Royal Institute of British Architects (RIBA) which is the most important of the architects' professional bodies.[4] Both the board and the RIBA have prescribed codes of conduct[5] and the RIBA produces the most important form of contract, the RIBA Standard Form of Agreement.

The term 'engineer' can be applied to so many different professionals in so many different situations that it is incapable of precise definition. Commonly engineers in the construction industry have been defined as non-architects carrying out professional duties analogous to those of architects.[6] However, very often the engineer will operate in a more limited role than the architect, bringing to bear a special expertise not generally found in the architect's profession, for example civil, structural or mechanical engineers and engineers, and architects frequently work together on construction projects, each contributing in his own area of expertise. Whilst not as tightly regulated as architects, there are a number of important professional bodies, and in particular the Institution of Civil Engineers (ICE), membership of which enables a person to describe himself as a Chartered Civil Engineer, whilst the

---

2 Section 20 of the Architects Act 1997.
3 The Act covers architects employed by others but does not cover those who operate occasionally or as a hobby. Bodies corporate, firms or partnerships are covered in the same way as individuals.
4 Note should also be made of the Association of Consultant Architects, which is made up of consultant architects in private practice.
5 It should also be noted that both bodies exercise disciplinary functions over their members, whilst the RIBA runs a conciliation scheme for those dissatisfied with the services of a member architect.
6 See the definitions in Jackson and Powell, *Professional Negligence* (fifth edition), para. 8–003, and D. Keating, *Law and Practice of Building Contracts* (seventh edition), para. 13–112.

Engineering Council is the national registration authority for professional engineers.[7] The ICE operates a code of professional standards and by-laws and is responsible for publishing one of the major forms of civil engineering contract, the ICE Conditions. The Association of Consulting Engineers (ACE) is the United Kingdom's leading trade association for engineering, technical and management consultancies with approximately 650 member firms. It produces the ACE suite of contracts.

Architects' and engineers' contracts

There is no legal requirement for architects to contract in any particular form and the normal laws of contract will apply to any agreement between an architect and his client. Thus although it is prudent for such agreements to be in writing, or at least evidenced by an exchange of correspondence, agreements are often oral or partially in writing and partially oral. Similarly, although it is prudent for all terms of a contract to be agreed before the commencement of services it is common practice for the substantial terms to be agreed at the outset and for remaining matters to be implied according to custom and practice or to be agreed subsequently. This is notwithstanding the requirements in paragraph 2.7 of the RIBA Code of Conduct that a member should undertake:

> when making an engagement, whether by an agreement for professional services, by a contract of employment or by a contract for the supply of services and goods, to state whether or not professional indemnity insurance is held and to have defined beyond reasonable doubt and recorded the terms of the engagement including the scope of the service, the allocation of responsibilities and any limitation of liability, the method of calculation of remuneration and the provision for termination and adjudication.

The RIBA publishes a number of versions of the 'Standard Form of Agreement for the Appointment of an Architect'[8] which now from the basis of most traditional contracts. The RIBA Standard Form of Agreement for the Appointment of an Architect (SFA/99) is attached at Appendix 2. It will be noted that the structure of the agreement is to set out the identities of the parties, a description of the project, the precise nature of the services to be provided by the architect, the fees and expenses to be paid (usually on a work stage basis), any additional services, all of which is followed by quite lengthy

---

7 Other important professional bodies include the Institution of Structural Engineers (I Struct E), the Institution of Mechanical Engineers (I Mech E) and the Institution of Electrical Engineers (IEE).

8 See *A Guide to the RIBA Forms of Appointment 1999* (RIBA 1999) which explains the differences between the different forms.

conditions of engagement. However, in relation to very substantial projects and in relation to design-and-build contracts it is common for bespoke contracts to be employed.

Consideration of the contract is the starting point for an appreciation of the architect's obligations to his client. Each contract will of course vary, depending on the circumstances. However, the following common features, relevant to scope of duty, should be noted.

The identification of the services to be performed

It is particularly important for architects accurately to define the extent of their services. On a traditional contract this may be straightforward. However, for a more complicated or unusual contract there is often a risk that failure accurately to define roles and responsibilities will lead to future disputes.[9] Frequently problems arise during the job as to responsibility for the work of other professionals and consequently care should also be taken to ensure that these responsibilities continue to be clearly recorded. In *Richard Roberts Holdings Ltd* v. *Douglas Smith Stimson Partnership*[10] the defendant architects believed that they had discharged their duty to the employer by introducing him to a contractor supplying tank linings. When the linings failed they declined to accept responsibility. However, the court held that the architects' responsibility extended to the whole of the works and thus included the supervision of the lining works.

The obligation to use reasonable skill and care

An architect's written contract will invariably contain an express term that the architect should exercise 'reasonable skill and care'.[11] In the absence of an express term – for example because the contract is oral or is only partially recorded in writing – an obligation to carry out the architects' services with reasonable skill and care will be implied by law.[12] It is open to the parties to attempt to agree an obligation for some higher degree of skill and care. This is sometimes seen in the use of phrases such as 'utmost skill and care' and 'highest degree of skill and care'. However, in practice such phrases do not tend to add to the architect's obligations, as the courts find too difficult to

---

9 One of the most frequent disputes is whether an architect who has undertaken the responsibility to design works has also undertaken the responsibility to supervise their construction. This was one of the key issues in *Tesco* v. *Norman Hitchcock Partnership* (1997) 56 Con LR 42.
10 (1988) 46 BLR 50.
11 In clause 2 (1) of the RIBA SFA/99 the obligation is expressed as 'The Architect shall in performing the services and discharging the obligations under [this Agreement] exercise reasonable skill and care in conformity with the normal standards of an architect's profession.'
12 Section 13 of the Supply of Goods and Services Act 1982.

decide what these phases mean. In practical terms, unless an architect agrees to guarantee that his design will work in a certain way or the building will be constructed to a certain cost (see below) the benchmark by which his performance is to be judged is the exercise of such reasonable skill and care as would be exercised by a reasonably competent member of his profession.

Other obligations

It is open to an architect not merely to agree to exercise reasonable skill and care but to guarantee that his design will perform to a particular standard. Such warranties are comparatively rare because of the very onerous obligations they place upon the architect: the architect is guaranteeing that irrespective of circumstances beyond his control his design will perform to a particular standard come what may. In the absence of a clear agreement to provide a warranty the courts occasionally decide that on the facts of a particular case (and irrespective of the architect's duty of reasonable skill and care) the architect has provided a warranty that his design will be 'reasonably fit for the purpose for which it is intended'.[13] Such case are rare and will generally be confined to circumstances where the court finds that, because of the particular importance of way in which the design was intended to function, the importance which the employer attached to its success and the claims that the architect made on its behalf, the parties intended that such an obligation should exist.[14]

Engineers' contracts

As with architects, there is no legal requirement for a particular form of contract to be entered into by an engineer, although it is common for various types of standard form to be employed. The most commonly employed are the ACE Conditions of Engagement which come in a number of variations which illustrate the breadth of responsibilities commonly accorded to engineers. Sometimes distinguishing between civil and mechanical/electrical engineering, they cover arrangements where the engineer is lead consultant, not lead consultant but directly engaged by the client, where he provides design services of a design-and-construct contractor, where he provides reporting and advisory services, where he is a project manager and where he is a planning supervisor in accordance with the Construction (Design and Management) Regulations 1994. Additional variations cover minor works and sub-consultancy cases. Attached at Appendix 3 are excerpts from the ACE Conditions of Engagement Agreement A (1) [2002] for use where the consulting engineer is engaged as lead consultant. The

---

13 See *IBA* v. *EMI and BICC* (1980) 14 BLR 1.
14 See *George Hawkins* v. *Chrysler (UK)* (1986) 38 BLR 36.

structure of the Conditions of Engagement is that they commence with a memorandum of understanding which identifies the parties. This is followed by the conditions of engagement themselves and after these there are set out the services which the engineer provides. Although the engineer's responsibilities will generally be clear, as with architects it is important to define these obligations accurately. Similarly although it is open to an engineer to warrant that works of his design or constructed under his supervision will perform to a certain standard, such obligations are rare and the usual professional negligence dispute concerns the engineer's performance of his obligation to use reasonable skill and care.[15]

Reasonable skill and care

The vast majority of professional negligence actions concerning architects involve consideration of the duty of skill and care: did the architect exercise the reasonable skill and care to be expected of a member of his profession? The application of this standard was more fully explained by Windeyer J in the Australian case of *Voli* v. *Inglewood Shire Council*:[16]

> An architect undertaking any work in the way of his profession accepts the ordinary liabilities of any man who follows a skilled calling. He is bound to exercise due care, skill and diligence. He is not required to have an extraordinary degree of skill or the highest professional attainments. But he must bring to bear to the task he undertakes the competence and skill that is usual among architects practising their profession. And he must use due care. If he fails in these matters and the person who employed him thereby suffers damage, he is liable to that person.

In *Eckersly* v. *Binnie & Partners*,[17] in a passage which could be applied equally to any construction professional, Bingham LJ commented on the required standard of performance for consulting engineers thus:

> A professional man should command the corpus of knowledge which forms part of the professional equipment of the ordinary member of his profession. He should not lag behind other ordinarily assiduous and intelligent members of his profession in knowledge of new advances, discoveries and developments in his field. He should be alert to the hazards and risks inherent in any professional task he undertakes to the extent that other ordinarily competent members of the profession

15 Again this duty will be implied by law if not expressly contained within the contract. In the ACE Conditions of Engagement it is contained at para. 2.4.
16 [1963] ALR 657 at 661.
17 (1988) 18 Con LR 1.

would be alert. He must bring to any professional task he undertakes no less expertise, skill and care than other ordinarily competent members would bring but need bring no more. The standard is that of the reasonable average. The law does not require of a professional man that he be a paragon combining the qualities of polymath and prophet.

It will be noted that in setting the standard of skill and care to be expected of architects and engineers the courts do not differentiate between those professionals at the height of their profession carrying out substantial multi-million-pound contracts and those engaged at a more mundane level, perhaps in relation to very low-budget projects.[18] This is because the courts view each case on its merits and decide whether the professional fell below the requisite standard of care in that case. In cases where it is clear that no reasonably competent architect or engineer could have advised as he did, it is irrelevant that the professional was either the senior partner of a substantial and well respected practice or an unqualified person practising as an architect.[19] However, where an engineer holds himself out as a specialist in a particular field he will be judged by the standard of the reasonably competent specialist in that field. Moreover the sophistication of both the professional and the employer undoubtedly affects the decision in marginal cases. Whilst the courts rarely accept that the application of the standard is affected,[20] employers of sophisticated and highly experienced professionals will generally receive a more sympathetic hearing when contending that the architect or engineer should have been aware of some obscure risk.[21]

In contrast, the sophistication and resources of the employer are a feature which the courts are openly willing to consider when deciding whether the reasonably skilful professional was obliged to give certain advice. In *J. Jarvis & Sons Ltd* v. *Castle Wharf Developments Ltd*[22] architects engaged by a developer found their contracts novated to a contractor which gave instructions for a different scheme. Subsequently the contractor discovered that the works contravened planning permission. The contractor alleged that the architect should have advised it at the commencement of the novation that its new scheme did not comply. The Court of Appeal accepted the architect's

18 See for example *Wimpey Construction UK Ltd* v. *Poole* [1984] 2 Lloyds Rep 499.
19 As was the case in *Cardy* v. *Taylor* (1994) 38 Con LR 79.
20 Rare examples include *Brown* v. *Gilbert-Scott and another* (1995) 35 Con LR 120 where the court was influenced by the client's repeated attempts radically to reduce the architect's budget.
21 Thus in *Greaves & Co. (Contractors) Ltd* v. *Baynham Meikle & Partners* [1974] 1 WLR 1261 the court at first instance held that although the defendant engineers had acted in accordance with the commonly accepted practice of a substantial body of the profession, they owed a higher duty to the employer. The Court of Appeal reversed this finding but held that what the judge meant was that notwithstanding the divergence of professional opinion 'special steps' were necessary to discharge the engineers' duty on the particular facts.
22 [2001] Lloyds Rep PN 308.

submission that, in the absence of any express or implied request for advice, a construction professional has a duty to provide unsolicited advice only when his reasonable perception of his client's skill and experience suggests that his client needs such advice. In this case the contractor was a substantial and experienced design-and-build contractor and the architects were entitled to assume that it had informed itself of the planning position.[23]

As is explained in Chapter 1, the courts will almost always consider expert evidence when deciding whether an architect or engineer acted with reasonable competence. Stephen Brown LJ explained the role of this evidence in *Nye Saunders & Partners* v. *Alan E. Bristow*:[24]

> Where there is a conflict as to whether he has discharged that duty, the courts approach the matter upon the basis of considering whether there was evidence that at the time a responsible body of architects would have taken the view that the way in which the subject of enquiry had carried out his duties was an appropriate way of carrying out the duty, and would not hold him guilty of negligence merely because there was a body of competent professional opinion that he was at fault.

The body of expertise available with reference to the professions of both architects and engineers is partly recorded in codes of practice and similar professional standards. Beyond these such codes, at least in the United Kingdom, building regulations and other statutory requirements add a further layer of reference. Failure to comply with these codes frequently forms the basis of allegations of professional negligence and, although many are sufficiently broad to allow flexibility in interpretation,[25] a failure, once proven, is *prima facie* evidence of breach of duty.[26] However, the codes are no more than a guide and an architect or engineer who slavishly follows them when it is inappropriate to do so may also be found to have acted in breach of duty.[27]

23 But this case should not be taken to establish that there is a lower standard of care in every instance where the employer is experienced. *In Gloucestershire Health Authority* v. *Torpy* (1997) 55 Con LR 124 the court rejected an argument by mechanical services engineers that on the facts of their case the employer's experience and knowledge had any effect on their standard of performance.
24 (1987) 37 BLR 92 at 103.
25 Further it is important to judge them as they would be interpreted by the profession and not by lawyers – see HH Judge Lloyd QC in *J. Sainsbury plc* v. *Broadway Malayan* [1999] PNLR 286 at 302, 303.
26 See the New Zealand case of *Bevan Investments Ltd* v. *Blackhall and Struthers* (No. 2) [1973] 2 NZLR 45.
27 See *Holland & Hannen and Cubitts (Northern) Ltd* v. *Welsh Health Technical Services Organisation* (1985) 35 Build LR 1, where the novel design concept meant that the codes were of limited utility.

Examples

Knowledge of the law

An architect must have sufficient knowledge of those principles of law relevant to his professional practice in order reasonably to protect his client from damage and loss. Such areas might include the application of building regulations or certain aspects of common building contracts. However, the most frequent instance of this principle is in relation to planning. In *BL Holdings Ltd* v. *Robert J. Wood & Partners*[28] the employer engaged the architects to obtain planning permission for an office block. The architects were misled by a planning official into believing that a development permit was not required. When the true situation was discovered – and planning permission declared null and void – it took the employer three years to rectify the situation. At first instance the court decided that the architects had been negligent. Although this decision was overturned on appeal, it is clear that had the architects simply misunderstood the law on planning, as opposed to being misled, there would have been no defence to the charge of breach of duty. Indeed it has been held that a cautious and necessarily time-consuming approach to consultation with the planning authorities can be an appropriate strategy even where the employer suffers delays as a result. In *Hancock* v. *Turner*[29] the court refused to criticise architects who had unofficially submitted four different schemes to planners during a period when the value of the proposed development was falling. On the particular facts of that development, the architects were right to be cautious. As with other areas of practice, where an architect reaches the limits of his expertise he may be obliged to advise the employer that he should obtain specialist planning advice.

Similarly where the architect becomes aware or (or has reason to suspect the existence of) private law restrictions such as easements or restrictive covenants it is incumbent upon him to draw these to the attention of his employer even if he lacks the expertise to evaluate them himself. Where, as often happens, an architect or engineer is required to interpret building regulations the court will strive to apply the test of whether a reasonably competent architect or engineer could have interpreted the regulations, as has happened.

> The interpretation of Building Regulations is ultimately a question of law; but it is relevant to consider how they strike the non-lawyers, such as engineers, for whom they are intended and who have to understand and apply them. It does not of course follow that if the correct meaning is not recognised by such a reasonably competent professional person then that person is negligent.[30]

28 (1978) 10 BLR 48.
29 [1999] PNLR 814.
30 *J. Sainsbury* v. *Broadway Malayan* [1999] PNLR 286 per HH Humphrey Lloyd QC at 302.

Examination of the site

Generally speaking an architect or engineer will be engaged at the inception of a project. For both architects and engineers, thorough examination of the site is as least as important as an understanding of the legal restrictions for development. In the first place reasonable care must be taken in measuring the site. Especially where the site is likely to be constricted or where accurate measurement is otherwise important it is essential that the architect or engineer does not merely rely upon information provided by others but carries out the measurement himself. Thus in *Columbus Co.* v. *Clowes*[31] the architect negligently relied upon site measurement information provided by a third party with the result that the site was too small for the intended development. Even where site measurement information comes from the employer or his agent, care should be taken either to ensure that the information is accurate or to ensure that the employer accepts responsibility for its accuracy.[32]

Secondly it is important to ascertain the nature of the ground conditions – usually a task which will involve the employment of a specialist contractor. In *Eames London Estates Ltd* v. *North Hertfordshire District Council*[33] although the architect knew that the proposed building was to be sited on made ground he failed to make any enquiries as to whether the foundations would be adequate for the loading (assuming that they would be because the site was an old railway embankment). In the event the foundations failed and the architect was held to have been negligent in specifying the loading for the piers without any adequate attempt to ascertain whether the ground was suitable for the loading. In *City of Bradford* v. *Kemp and Wallace-Caruthers & Associates Ltd*[34] the site for a new hall and fire station was to be over an old rubbish tip. No doubt encouraged by commercial pressures the defendant engineers recommended a design whereby only the main walls were supported on piles (the partition walls being supported by the floors laid on granular fill) rather than a system entirely supported by piling. Although there were limited sample tests, they were inadequate to demonstrate that the system was safe. It failed and the Ontario Court of Appeal held that the engineers were negligent in not carrying out proper surveys.

Moreover such surveys as are carried out must be appropriate to ascertain the risks. In *Moneypenny* v. *Hartland*[35] the engineer was held liable to his employer because although his original investigations had been adequate he had then altered the proposed location of the building. Nor does risk necessarily arise at the construction stage. In *Kaliszewska* v. *John Clague &*

---

31 [1903] 1 KB 244.
32 See *Cardy* v. *Taylor* (1994) 38 Con LR 79 where the contractor's information was not merely inaccurate but was inconsistent with other information in the possession of the architect.
33 (1980) 259 EG 491.
34 (1960) 23 DLR (2d) 641.
35 (1824) 1 Car & P 351.

Partners[36] the architect was held liable for failing to anticipate that removal of trees would lead to heave, damaging the building on site.

Estimates

Providing costs estimates, budgets and other estimates is an increasingly important part of the architect's functions (and, to a much lesser extent, those of the engineer). They are a frequent source of dispute between the architect or engineer and the employer in cases where the costs of projects overrun. As with all other areas of professional expertise the architect is required to use reasonable skill and care in producing the estimates. Failure to exercise such care may lead to the architect losing his fees or even – if loss can be shown – paying damages. In *Nye Saunders & Partners* v. *Alan E. Bristow*[37] the employer asked for an estimate for the cost of renovating his mansion. Having consulted a quantity surveyor the architects estimated £238,000. However, no allowance was made for the effects of inflation (these events taking place in a period of high inflation). By the time that contractors were engaged the cost estimate had risen to £440,000. The employer cancelled the project and refused to pay the architects' fees. The court held that the architects were negligent, as they should have warned that their estimate took no account of inflation. However, the mere fact of a very substantial over-spend does not of itself prove than an estimation was negligent. In *Copthorne Hotel (Newcastle) Ltd* v. *Arup Associates*[38] although the out-turn piling costs were £975,000 as against the estimated £425,000 HH Judge Hicks held that the disparity, of itself, was insufficient to establish breach of duty. Evidence was required that defendant's methodology had been faulty.

In addition to cost estimates architects are often required to estimate certain performance criteria or features of the building to be constructed. These can be as mundane as the active life of the escalators. However, they can also be of critical importance to the client, as in *Gable House Estates* v. *Halpern Partnership*.[39] The employers in this case were the owners of an office building in central London. Their options were to sell the building or to redevelop it and let it. The architects, as lead consultants, were responsible for the provision of cost plans prepared by the quantity surveyors which included schedules showing the amount of 'lettable space' as being 34,000 sq. ft. Relying on this information, the employer decided to proceed with the re-development option. In fact there was only 32,000 sq. ft of lettable space and the court found that the architects negligently failed to warn that their estimation of the usable office space was very approximate and failed to warn as to a distinction between usable space and lettable space.

---

36 (1984) 5 Con LR 62.
37 (1987) 37 Build LR 92.
38 (1996) 58 Con LR 105.
39 (1995) 48 Con LR 1.

Design

Except in special cases the architect or engineer does not warrant that his design will achieve a particular result, but he is under an obligation to prepare the design with reasonable skill and care. The starting point for consideration of this obligation is the employer's instructions: has the architect or engineer provided the design he was instructed to provide? Particularly with relatively inexperienced clients this imposes an obligation on the architect to ensure that he understands exactly what the employer wants him to design and has explored with the employer exactly that the design is intended to provide. In *Stormont Main Working Men's Club* v. *J. Roscoe Milne Partnership*[40] the employer asked the architect to design an extension of the working men's club but then complained that the design was defective because the position of the pillars did not allow for snooker matches at national competition level. The allegation failed because the court found that the employer had no intention of creating facilities for playing competition snooker, still less had he led the architects to believe that that was what he wanted. However, had this been the employer's genuine intention it is likely that the architects would have been in breach of duty had they failed to explore with him the implications of their design. Similarly where the employer requests changes in the design during the course of construction it is important for the architect to explore the consequences of these with him and in particular to point out consequences which he as a layman could not be expected to foresee.

The mere fact that an employer has approved a design is not a defence to allegations of breach of duty should that design subsequently prove to be defective. Only if the potential for defects has been fully recognised by the architect and fully explained to the employer is the latter's approval likely to provide a defence. In certain situations – particularly when employed by an experienced and sophisticated employer – it may be sufficient for the architect or engineer to warn that the consequences of a particular instruction are unclear and have not been fully evaluated. Alternatively the limitations of the design may be so clear that there is no requirement of a warning. In *Worboys* v. *Acme Investments*[41] it was held that the omission of downstairs lavatories in plans for a housing development would have been sufficiently clear to the experienced property developer employer. However, even in these circumstances the architect or engineer should take care to ensure that, in so far as is necessary, the employer is aware of the gravity of the risk he runs. By the same token it is no defence to an architect or an engineer whose design has proved to be defective for him to assert that it was inspected and approved by local authority building control inspectors or other statutory bodies.[42]

40 (1988) 13 Con LR 126.
41 (1969) 4 BLR 136.
42 See *Voli* v. *Inglewood Shire Council* [1963] ALR 657 where the High Court of Australia ruled that it was no defence that the Public Works Department had inspected and passed the design of a stage which subsequently collapsed.

Similarly it will generally be no defence that some other professional engaged by the employer has inspected the design and approved it.

The failure of what should have been a relatively straightforward design will generally be grounds for asserting that the design professional was negligent. In theory it is a defence to an allegation of breach of duty giving rise to defective design that the design was so revolutionary and untested that it could fail notwithstanding the exercise of reasonable skill and care. In *Turner* v. *Garland and Christopher*[43] Erle J directed the jury as follows:

> You should bear in mind that if the building is of an ordinary description, in which he [the architect] has an abundance of experience, and it proved a failure, this is evidence of a want of skill and attention. But, if out of the ordinary course, and you employ him about a novel thing, about which he has little experience, if it has not had the test of experience, failure may be consistent with skill. The history of all great improvements shows failure of those who embark in them. . . .

However, in practice it is rare for architects or engineers to succeed in a defence that because the design was novel any defect in it could not be attributed to a breach of duty on their part. Indeed in most cases where a novel design is in issue, the Courts are alert to failure on the part of the architects or engineers to advise of the risks of such designs and in particular as to the desirability of extensive testing.[44] Frequently designs are found to be defective because the architect or engineer has not considered the practical consequences of the materials to be employed or the way in which the structure is to be erected and then maintained. Thus in *Pride Valley Foods Ltd* v. *Hall & Partners (Contract Management) Ltd*[45] the project managers engaged for the design and construction of a bread-making factory were found to be liable for failing to warn the employer that the expanded polystyrene panels which he wished to use in order to reduce costs were highly flammable and if ignited could lead to a rapidly spreading fire. In *Michael Hyde & Associates Ltd* v. *J.D. Williams & Co. Ltd*[46] the architects failed to make sufficient enquiries as to the operation of the gas heating system which they recommended to the employer, with the result that the employer's textiles were discoloured. By contrast in *George Hawkins* v. *Chrysler (UK)*[47] an engineer was found not to have been negligent despite the fact that the shower room tiles he selected proved slippery when wet because he had made careful investigation of RIBA data sheets and trade brochures and had consulted an experienced specialist flooring firm. Where the design causes the employer

43 (1853) cited in *Hudson's Building Contracts* (fourth edition) Vol II, p. 1.
44 See, for example, *Victoria University of Manchester* v. *Hugh Wilson* [1984] 2 Con LR 43.
45 (2001) 76 Con LR 1.
46 [2001] PNLR 233.
47 (1986) 38 BLR 36.

unforeseen expense, in that it proves unnecessarily difficult to construct, the architect or engineer may be breach of duty. In *Equitable Debenture Assets Corp. Ltd* v. *William Moss Group Ltd*[48] HH Judge Newey said:

> I think that if the implementation of part of a design requires work to be carried out on site, the designer should ensure that the work can be performed by those likely to be employed to do it, in the conditions which can be foreseen, the exercise of the care and skill ordinarily to be expected by them. If the work would demand exceptional skill, and particularly if it would have to be performed partly from scaffolding and often in windy conditions, then the design will lack what the experts in evidence describe as 'buildability.' Similarly I think that if a design requires work to be carried out on site in such a way that those whose duty it is to supervise it and/or check that it has been done will encounter greater difficulty in doing so, then the design will again be defective. It may perhaps be described as lacking 'supervisability.'

In this context it should be noted that since the introduction of the Construction (Design and Management) Regulations 1994 the designer is required, in respect of larger projects, to have regard to the health and safety of persons carrying out the construction work. The notion of practicality as a test of design extends beyond the construction phase. Design which proves unnecessarily expensive or difficult to maintain – for example windows which can be cleaned only by the use of abseilers or mechanical plant which requires a complete shut-down for localised repairs – is likely to be defective unless the employer has been warned of the consequences and has accepted them.

Responsibility for the work of others

One of the most fertile sources of actions against architects and engineers is their responsibility for and/or reliance upon the work of other professionals. With the increasing complexity of contracts and specialisation of building professionals the extent to which an architect or engineer can safely rely upon the work of other professionals has become an important issue for them and their employers. This topic raises three questions:

1   To what extent can an architect or engineer become liable for defective work which partly results from the work of other professionals engaged by the employer?
2   To what extent has the architect or engineer a duty to warn the employer concerning the shortcomings of other professionals engaged by him?

48 (1984) 2 Con LR 1 at 21.

3   In what circumstances will it be a defence to an architect or an engineer
     to contend that he relied upon the advice or work of specialists (or even
     delegated the performance of some tasks to them)?

As stated above, one of the principal reasons why care should be taken in
describing the scope of the architect's or engineer's duty under the contract
is that it may help avoid disputes as to whether that professional is liable
for some subsequent failure in the works. A prominent example is *Holland
& Hannen and Cubitts (North) Ltd* v. *Welsh Health Technical Services
Organisation*[49] where the architects and engineers were in dispute as to
responsibility for the failure of the floors, which suffered from deflection.
The Court of Appeal, by a majority, decided that as between them the responsibility lay with the architects, as the deflections were unsatisfactory from a
visual and/or aesthetic standpoint and that matters of visual or aesthetic
fitness (as opposed to structural fitness) were properly within the province
of the architect. The decision does not establish any principle of general
application because the roles and responsibilities of all the professionals
involved were determined on the basis of the court's view of their relations
in that case. Moreover that decision was unusual in absolving one of the
professionals entirely. In the typical case the court will apportion liability
with neither party escaping altogether.

   In the absence of some express obligation to do so,[50] an architect or
engineer is not obliged to report on the failings of another professional unless
the danger or risk ought to be apparent to that architect or engineer. In
Investors in Industry v. *South Bedfordshire District Council*[51] the architects
were contractually required to appoint independent specialists but were
expressly not made responsible for their work. On that basis the Court of
Appeal held that the architect's responsibility was confined to giving general
direction. However, this was subject to one important qualification:

> If any danger or problem arises in connection with the work allotted to
> the expert, of which an architect of reasonable competence ought to be
> aware and reasonably could be expected to warn the client . . . the duty
> of the architect [is] to warn the client. In such a contingency he is not
> entitled to rely blindly on the expert.

Of course this raises the question 'When is a danger sufficiently apparent that
an architect of reasonable competence could be expected to warn the client?'
Each case is likely to be determined on its particular facts; however, as a

49 (1985) 35 BLR 1.
50 Some contracts require the architect or engineer to co-ordinate their design with that of
    other professionals. This probably imparts a duty to check that nothing in the other
    professional's design is inimicable to that being produced by the professional.
51 (1985) 32 BLR 1.

general guide, the more specialist the nature of the work undertaken by the 'expert' the less likely it is that a reasonably competent architect or engineer would be alerted to the risk. Moreover in many situations it may be a satisfactory discharge of the architect's duties if, having considered the possibility of a risk, he makes careful enquiries of the expert and receives satisfactory (albeit incorrect) answers.

The most common difficulty for both architects and engineers in relation to other professionals arises when the architect or engineer themselves rely upon the services of an expert to carry out their work. Typically an architect might recommend the engagement the services of a structural engineer to calculate loadings, or an engineer might recommend the retention of a soil consultant to analyse samples. In the event that that professional's work is defective and this causes loss to the employer, is the architect or engineer liable for that loss or can he defend himself by saying that he reasonably relied upon the services of the expert? Under the RIBA conditions the architect is absolved from responsibility provided that he acted reasonably in recommending the appointment of and relying upon the expert.[52] The position is probably the same at common law and under most engineering contracts. However, suppose that the architect or engineer engages the professional directly, without the express or implied permission of the employer, and thus effectively subcontracts part of his work. In that situation it is difficult to see how the architect or engineer will escape liability for the consequences of mistakes made by the expert he has retained.[53] It may be that in an exceptional case the court would hold that the architect or engineer had no option, in practice, but to rely upon the expert and that consequently could not be said to have acted without reasonable care.[54] However, in the generality of cases an architect or engineer who delegates part of his function to another expert without the express approval of the employer is likely to be held liable for the consequences of the mistakes of that expert.

Of course these situations should be distinguished from that where an architect or engineer is appointed the lead consultant or for some other reason is required to co-ordinate the work of other design professionals. Here any defect in the works which arises as a result of lack of co-ordination (as opposed to any inherent want of skill in the preparation of the design itself) is likely to be attributed to a breach of duty on the part of the architect or engineer. This is a common failing where the architect or engineer engages a specialist designer in relation to a discrete part of the works and thereafter neglects to give that part of the works sufficient attention. Thus in *Equitable*

---

52 *Investors in Industry* v. *South Bedfordshire District Council* (1985) 32 BLR 1.
53 See *Moresk Cleaners Ltd* v. *Hicks* [1966] 2 Lloyds Rep 338.
54 This may be the explanation of the decision in *Merton London Borough Council* v. *Lowe* (1981) 18 BLR 130 where the architects had no practicable option but to rely upon the recommendation of the supplier of the ceiling mix, which was the nominated subcontractor for the ceiling works.

Debenture Assets Corp. Ltd v. *William Moss Group Ltd*[55] defects in the curtain walling were held to have been caused by failure on the part of the architects to co-ordinate the work of the specialist curtain walling consultants with the work of the curtain walling subcontractor, the architects having assumed that the specialist consultants would carry out sufficient co-ordination without their prompting.

Preparation of the building contract

Preparation of a building contract can involve the architect or engineer in advising on the choice and terms of the contract, preparation of the contract documents (including having at least an oversight role into the preparation of a bill of quantities) and advising upon and overseeing the tender process and engagement of the contractor. Depending on the nature of the works and the size and sophistication of the employer, the architect or engineer may be called upon to give what amounts to commercial advice in respect of these functions. Although it is now rare, architects have been held to be in breach of duty to their employers for failing to advise that even quite modest projects should be put out to competitive tender.[56] The inexperienced client will almost certainly require advice as to the appropriate form of contract to be employed and his rights and obligations under that contract. In particular the architect or engineer will need to explain the role of nominated subcontractors (if any) and the desirability of obtaining direct warranties as to the quality of that subcontractor's work. Prior to the recommendation of any contractor an architect should make enquiries not merely as to his capability but, perhaps as important, as to his solvency. Thus in *Partridge* v. *Morris*[57] the court held that prior to advising as to the acceptability of tenders the architect should have advised his inexperienced client as to the solvency of the contractors. In order to do this he could have made enquiries of building merchants, obtained bank references, obtained trade credit references, made enquiries of other architects, arranged for a company search or asked the contractors to provide copies of their accounts. Some projects may be sufficiently large to justify the contractor being asked to provide a bond or parent company guarantee. In *Convent Hospital* v. *Eberlin & Partners*[58] the employers successfully sued the architects for failing to obtain a performance bond from the contractor, who subsequently became insolvent. An architect or engineer advising on the retention of contractors should generally ensure that any contractor carries appropriate insurance. In *Pozzolanic Lytag* v. *Bryan Hobson Associates*[59] the contractors who designed and built storage

---

55 (1984) 2 Con LR 1.
56 See *Hutchinson* v. *Harris*, reported at appeal in [1978] 10 BLR 19.
57 [1995] CILL 1095.
58 See (1989) 14 Con LR 1.
59 [1999] BLR 267.

facilities for pulverised fuel ash were required by the contract to carry insurance protecting the employer in the event of certain losses arising from design defects. Part of the works collapsed owing to defective design and the contractors were found to be without insurance. The court ruled that the engineers who were project managers should have made sure that adequate insurance was in place. It was no defence for the engineers to argue that they did not have the expertise to judge the adequacy of the insurance: they should either have sought legal advice or expressly advised the employer that they did not know whether the contractor's insurance was adequate.

Administration of a building contract

Architects and engineers are frequently employed to administer building contracts. All the standard forms of contract provide for a named architect or engineer or provide for a person acting as the employer's representative who is invariably an architect or engineer. The functions carried out in this role chiefly comprise the inspection of works, the issuing of payment certificates, the issuing of instructions (particularly as to variations), making decisions on the contractor's claims for extensions of time and delay and disruption, giving instructions as to the remedying of defective work and determining practical completion. The extensive body of law which has evolved concerning the proper exercise of these functions concerns actions taken by contractors against employers and is beyond the scope of this book. However, it is important to note that just as the contractor may suffer by reason of a failure on the part of the architect or engineer adequately to perform his duties, so too the employer may suffer loss because the contractor has been overpaid or his work has not been subjected to proper scrutiny. Even where the contractor is the aggrieved party, the very fact of his bringing legal proceedings against the employer may lead to the latter suffering loss which would have been avoided had the architect or engineer carried out his functions with reasonable competence.

Particularly on a large project, where the architect or engineer may be acting as project manager, it is incumbent upon him to ensure that he organises the works so as to minimise delay and expense to his employer. In *Cornfield* v. *Grant*[60] the court found that the architect's failure properly to organise a building project caused it to be 'an inadequately controlled muddle' with consequential loss to the employer. Organisation encompasses the ability to respond efficiently to the difficulties which emerge on any construction project, particularly when they are not the fault of the contractor. If the architect or engineer is unable to respond with reasonable diligence and competence to late changes in the client's brief, emerging inconsistencies in the original design or changes required by statutory bodies the project

60 (1992) 29 Con LR 58.

is likely to be delayed, with resultant unnecessary expense to the employer. A further common source of difficulty in relation to design-and-build projects is the speed of design approvals which if delayed can cause damaging design holds. Of course this duty does not require the architect or engineer to advise the contractor as to how his work is to be carried out – that is a matter entirely within his province – but it is his function to ensure so far as he is able to do so that all impediments which are not the contractor's respon-sibility are removed or minimised.

Considerable care should be exercised in the issuing of notices and certifi-cates. Since the House of Lords' decision in *Sutcliffe* v. *Thackrah*[61] it has been possible for employers to sue architects and engineers for the negligent issue of final certificates (which may bind the employer as against the contractor). Of course errors of judgment and trivial errors may not amount to negligence. In particular the courts give considerable leeway to decisions which by their nature cannot be the expression of an exact science[62] – for example in relation to applications for an extension of time and additional payment for loss and expense – and to decisions which may involve difficult judgments – for example the issue of a notice of non-performance. In *Secretary of State for Transport* v. *Birse Farr Joint Venture*[63] the court held that the mere fact that the employer had been exposed to increased interest payments because of delays in certification by the engineers was insufficient to make out an action in professional negligence against them: there had to be 'some misapplication or misunderstanding of the contract by the engineer'. However, once an error has been shown to lie outside this margin of reasonable judgment the architect or engineer will be found to have acted in breach of duty and may be liable for any loss caused to the employer.

The architect or engineer is obliged to exercise sufficient supervision to ensure, as far as is reasonably possible, that the quality of the work matches up to the standard contemplated by the building contract. Of course what is adequate is a question of fact in each case. In *Cornfield* v. *Grant*[64] HH Judge Bowsher QC said:

> What is adequate by way of supervision and other works is not in the end to be tested by the number of hours worked on site or elsewhere, but by asking whether it was enough. At some stages of some jobs exclusive attention may be required to the job in question (either in the office or on site): at other stages of the same job, or during most of the duration of other jobs, it will be quite sufficient to give attention to the job only from time to time. The proof of the pudding is in the eating. Was the attention given enough for this particular job?

---

61 [1974] AC 727.
62 See generally *Sutcliffe* v. *Chippendale and Edmondson* (1971) 18 BLR 149.
63 (1993) 62 BLR 36.
64 (1992) 29 Con LR 58 at 58–9.

The mere fact that some defects escape the attention of the architect or engineer does not of itself indicate negligence: he cannot stand over the shoulder of every operative all of the time. However, he must pay particular attention to the key parts of the works at key times and in particular anticipate the areas where it is likely that, if defects occur, they will prove serious and/or difficult to uncover subsequently. In *Jameson* v. *Simon*[65] the architect had visited the works once a week, as was customary at the time. However, he failed to spot that the bottoming of the cement floor was made of waste. The court found he was in breach of duty and Lord Trayner said:

> It is contended that the architect cannot be constantly at the work, and this is obviously true. But he or someone representing him should undoubtedly see to the principal parts of the work before they are hid from view, and if need be I think he should require a contractor to give notice before an operation is to be done which will prevent his so inspecting an important part of the work so as to be able to give his certificates upon knowledge, and not an assumption, as to how the work hidden from view has been done.

The more critical the part of the works and the more risky its design the greater the obligation on the part of the architect or engineer to inspect closely.[66] Similarly if the architect has reason to doubt the competence of the contractor, or has experienced a higher than usual incidence of defects or even lack of candour on the part of the contractor or subcontractor, he may have good reason to devote more careful attention to inspections than would otherwise be the case.

Duties to third parties

Usually professional negligence disputes involving architects and engineers concern the performance of their contractual duties. Occasionally persons who have no contractual relationship with an architect or an engineer will wish to consider taking action against them. Whether and to what extent such actions can succeed will depend upon whether they can make out the existence of an actionable duty of care in tort (see Chapter 1) or bring themselves within the class of persons who have a right of action under statute. In either case such actions are uncommon and may be best discussed by reference to examples. However, where a duty of care (or similar statutory duty) is found to exist the test for breach of duty is exactly the same: did the architect or engineer act with the skill and care to be expected of a reasonably competent member of his profession?

---

65 [1899] 1 F (Ct of Sess) 1211, 1222.
66 See *George Fischer Holdings Ltd* v. *Multi Design Consultants Ltd* (1998)] 61 Con LR 85.

Persons injured by defective works

Architects and engineers owe a duty of care not to cause personal injury to anyone who they could reasonably foresee might be injured as a result of their negligence. In *Clay* v. *A. J. Crump & Sons Ltd*[67] a wall which was intended to be demolished was left as protection against intruders. The architect asked the demolition contractors whether the wall was safe but failed to inspect it himself. The wall subsequently collapsed, injuring a workman. He successfully sued the contractor, the demolition contractor and the architect. In *Targett* v. *Torfaen Borough Council*[68] a local authority that had designed and built a council house was held liable to a tenant who had been injured as a result of the negligent failure to provide a handrail and adequate lighting. However, as with a contractual duty of care, the mere fact that an injury has been caused by defective design or lack of supervision is not sufficient: it must be shown that the architect or engineer failed to exercise reasonable skill and care.

Purchasers of defective buildings

The purchaser of a building, who has no contractual connection with the architect or engineer, may discover that the design of that building is defective and that the architect or engineer was to blame. However, the law in the United Kingdom generally prevents that third party from recovering.[69] This is for reasons of public policy – the fact that the property is worth less than it should be is not sufficient reason to justify a right of action where no contractual relationship exists. It should be noted that this is not the law in Australia, Canada or New Zealand, and even in the United Kingdom it *may* be possible to claim where the defects are such as to cause actual or potential damage to other property, or is in respect of a recently completed dwelling house (see below) or has made the property dangerous to others. However, in the generality of cases it will be unlikely that the subsequent purchaser of a property will be able to take action against the architect or engineer who designed it.

Persons whose property is damaged by defective works to other property

An architect or engineer will generally owe a duty of care not to cause physical damage to property belonging to third parties *provided* this is different

---

67 [1964] 1 QB 533.
68 [1992] 3 AER 27.
69 Regard should be had to the discussion of this difficult topic in chapter 8 of Jackson and Powell, *Professional Negligence*, and in particular the survey of other Commonwealth jurisdictions.

property than that upon which he was working. Thus if an engineer negligently designs the ventilation systems for an office building so that it becomes too hot in midsummer, the owner of that office building, assuming he has no contractual relationship with the engineer, will be unable to sue him for the cost of remedial works. However, the owner may be able to sue for the cost of repairs to computer equipment located in the building which is damaged by the high temperatures. In *Bellefield Computer Services Ltd* v. *E. Turner & Sons Ltd*[70] a fire which had started in a storage area of a dairy processing plant spread through the plant because the internal fire-stop compartment wall to the storage area had been inadequately constructed. The builder, who had been engaged by the previous owner, had carried out work only on the storage area. The subsequent owner successfully sued the builder for the damage to the equipment and stock which were stored in the building, but not the fabric of the building itself, which, unlike the equipment and stock, was part of the same property as that upon which he had been working. However, even in this restricted application the courts have further cut down the scope of a duty of care. If the defect is 'patent' – that is, it could have been discovered by reasonably careful examination – no duty of care will lie. This is illustrated by the facts of *Baxall Securities Ltd and others* v. *Sheard and others*.[71] Sheard was a firm of architects retained by Berisford between 1989 and 1992 to design and supervise the construction of light industrial units. Baxall took a lease of the premises, but before so doing instructed a surveyor to carry out a survey. The survey indicated that that there was a problem with water ingress and the surveyors should have perceived that the overflow protection was inadequate. However, the survey did not identify a more fundamental design fault which could not have been identified by a reasonably careful inspection, namely the fact that the gutters were designed to deal with half the actual flow rate. There were two floods in May and September 1995 in which Baxall's goods stored in the premises were damaged. Baxall sued the architects in respect of both losses. At first instance Baxall succeeded on the losses from the second flood, which had been caused by the inadequate flow rate, but failed in respect of the first, which had been caused by the inadequate overflows. The architects owed a duty of care in respect of the flow rate, which was a latent defect, but not the overflows, which were patent. The Court of Appeal agreed with the court at first instance in respect of this analysis of the architect's duty of care. When is a defect 'patent?' Steel J in the Court of Appeal put it this way:

> Where in the normal course of events a surveyor would be engaged in a survey of a building for a purchaser, and, with the exercise of due diligence, that surveyor would have discovered a defect, that defect is

---

70 [2000] BLR 97.
71 [2001] BLR 36 and [2002] BLR 100.

patent whether or not a surveyor is in fact engaged and, if engaged, whether or not the surveyor performs his task competently.

However, it should be noted that the architects succeeded on causation. The Court of Appeal held that the fact that Baxall should have discovered the defect in the overflows was very relevant to the second flood. Had proper overflows been installed after the first flood the second flood would never have occurred.

Purchasers of defective dwelling houses

There is a statutory exception to the general rule that subsequent purchasers are unable to sue architects or engineers for defective design or workmanship. Under the Defective Premises Act 1972 (see Chapter 1) an architect or engineer who designs and/or supervises the construction of a dwelling house owes a subsequent purchaser a duty to see that it is constructed in a workmanlike manner, with proper materials and so that it is fit for habitation when completed.[72] If he is in breach of that duty the subsequent purchaser may sue the architect or engineer for damages. However, the value of this right of action to any subsequent purchaser is limited. In the first place the right only exists in respect of a dwelling house – that is, a house or a flat intended for human habitation. Secondly it is likely that in order to succeed the purchaser must show that property was rendered 'unfit for habitation'. Lastly the right to recover damage it ceases under the Limitation Act 1980 six years from the date of completion of the dwelling.

Persons who act in reliance on a representation

There may be situations where, although there is no contractual relationship, something said or done by an architect or an engineer causes a person to act in such a way that he suffers loss. An example might be a statement volunteered by an engineer that a particular part of a property would take a particular load, or the drawing up of plans by an architect with the knowledge that they might be relied upon by a person with whom the architect has no contract. In these circumstances the courts may hold that the architect or engineer owed a duty to that person to take reasonable care in making the statement or drawing up the plans and that any failure to exercise such care resulting in loss will give rise to a cause of action. In *Payne* v. *John Setchell Ltd*[73] the defendant civil and structural engineers gave the owner of recently constructed cottages certificates stating that the raft foundations were satisfactorily constructed and suitable for the support of the cottages.

---

72   The Act applies to all construction professionals.
73   [Unreported, 16 March 2001.]

The engineers knew that these certificates would be provided to prospective purchasers in order to encourage them to purchase. In fact the foundations were defective. Subsequent purchasers claimed to have relied upon the certificates when purchasing and sued the engineers for damages. The court found that because the engineers knew that the certificates would probably be relied upon by these purchasers they owed them a duty to take reasonable care and skill when completing them.

Contractors

Very occasionally a contractor may wish to take action against an architect or engineer for late or under-certification under a contract (typically when the employer has become insolvent). It is doubtful whether such an action could succeed,[74] although this cannot be ruled out as the courts will look at each case of this type on its merits.

Persons who are sued for losses also caused by the architect or engineer

It is very common in professional negligence actions for an architect or an engineer who is sued by an employer to seek to recover some of the loss from a fellow professional who was also engaged by the employer and who bears some of the responsibility for the loss or damage. By the same token it is very common for architects or engineers to have such 'contribution' proceedings taken against them by other professionals. Such proceedings arise not because of any duty owed to the fellow professional, but because the law permits a defendant to share the burden of any award of damages against him with any other person who is also responsible for the loss or injury. Reference should be made to Chapter 1. Under the Civil Liability Contributions Act 1978 the court will decide (1) whether the person from whom a contribution is sought is responsible for the same damage as is sought to be recovered from the person seeking a contribution and (2) if he is, the extent of the contribution which it is equitable for him to make. Thus where an employer sues an architect in relation to defects in a floor the architect may seek a contribution from the engineer on the basis that he was partly responsible for the defects. Assuming that the court finds that the floor was defective and that both the architect and the engineer were to blame it will then apportion any damages payable to the employer between the architect and the engineer. Such contributions are generally sought during the course of legal proceedings taken against the person seeking contribution, but can be taken up to two years after those proceedings have been resolved.

---

74 See *Pacific Associates Inc* v. *Baxter* [1990] 1 QB 193.

Practical considerations in claims against architects and engineers

Reference should be made to Chapter 7 for a full discussion of the practicalities of professional negligence actions against construction professionals. However, in respect of architects and engineers the following facts and matters should be kept in mind.

1 *Proving breach of duty.* In almost every instance it will be necessary for the person who proposes taking action against an architect or engineer to obtain an expert opinion form someone qualified and practising in that profession. This opinion will generally be required before proceedings are commenced. A professional defending such proceedings will generally also require an expert opinion.

2 *Insurance.* The adequacy of the professional's indemnity cover will often be a material consideration. All practising architects and engineers should carry professional indemnity insurance and are usually required to do so by the standard forms of contract if not the rules of their professional associations.

3 *Adjudication.* Although it is relatively uncommon for a claim against an architect or engineer to be referred to adjudication, this can and does happen. Most of the standard form agreements produced by the RIBA, ACE and other professional bodies provide for adjudication.

4 *Arbitration.* Architects and engineers can make provision in their contracts of engagement for any dispute arising between themselves and the employer to be referred to arbitration, but in practice litigation is often preferred. Potential claimants and defending professionals should be careful to check whether the contract contains a compulsory arbitration clause.

5 *Limitation of liability.* Just as an architect or engineer can agree to bear increased responsibilities, so he can attempt to limit his liability in the event that the employer seeks to claim compensation from him in respect of a breach of duty. Thus the RIBA Standard Form for the Appointment of an Architect SFA/99 provides the parties with the option of limiting the time within which an action against the architect may be brought, the amount of loss and damage and the way in which that loss and damage are calculated.[75] Similar provisions appear in the ACE Conditions of Engagement. Whilst such exclusion clauses may be challenged in law, it is likely that they will generally be upheld unless the architect has taken advantage of the employer's commercial inexperience to introduce unreasonable terms.[76]

---

75 Clauses 7.2 and 7.3.
76 See *Moores* v. *Yakeley* (1998) 62 Con LR 76 for a case where on the facts the imposition of a limitation clause was reasonable.

6 *Limitation periods.* As will all construction professionals, architects and engineers owe their employers a tortious duty of care which is usually the mirror image of the contractual duty of care. Employers may seek to rely upon the tortious duty in situations where, because more than six years has elapsed between the breach of duty and the commencement of proceedings, the claim in contract would be barred by the operation of Section 5 of the Limitation Act 1980 but the employer can none the less show that damage was first suffered within time or can rely upon Section 14A of that Act (see Chapter 1).

4 Quantity surveyors

Although quantity surveying is a relatively old profession, its nature has changed considerably as the nature of the construction industry has changed, particularly in response to increasing specialisation of roles demanded under many modern construction contracts. However, the core function of quantity surveyors remains that described in the nineteenth-century case of *Taylor* v. *Hall*,[1] namely 'taking out in detail the measurements and quantities from plans prepared by an architect for the purpose of enabling builders to calculate the estimates for which they would execute the plans.' Quantity surveyors are one branch of the wider family of surveyors which were, prior to 31 December 2000, divided into seven divisions by the Royal Institute of Chartered Surveyors, the others being commercial residential, building surveying, rural property, planning and development, land and hydrographic surveying and minerals surveying. After that date the seven divisions were replaced by sixteen faculties (each representing a particular surveying skill, one of which is construction management) and in respect of each a member may subscribe up to four. There is no statutory regulation of qualification and practice, although in order to become a 'chartered surveyor' the RICS requires certain qualifications and the passing of an 'Assessment of Professional Competence.' It operates a disciplinary code which makes professional indemnity insurance and continuing professional education compulsory and carries two levels of professional qualification, being Fellowship (FRICS) and Associate level (ARICS). It should be noted that whilst many of the older cases confuse quantity surveyors with building surveyors the latter division is now recognised as possessing distinct expertise in relation to the construction of buildings. Thus they commonly undertake design and inspection work (as would an architect) and have particular expertise in the interpretation and application of the building regulations. The RICS publishes a document entitled *Appointing a Quantity Surveyor* which consists of a guide for clients and surveyors, a standard form of enquiry setting out the details of the project together with the services which the

---

1 (1870) 4 IRCL 467 at 476.

quantity surveyor is to provide, followed by a fee offer which sets out the quantity surveyor's fees and lastly followed by the form of agreement which contains the terms of the appointment. The Form of Agreement [1992] is provided at Appendix 4.

The usual duties of a quantity surveyor

The usual duties of a quantity surveyor can be described by reference to different stages in a construction programme. At the outset and before a building contract is entered into a quantity surveyor may be engaged by the employer to advise him of the estimated cost of the project on the basis of the plans prepared. He will generally be asked to prepare the detailed bill of quantities and schedules to enable contractors to tender for the work. When the tenders are submitted he may be called upon to advise as to whether certain parts of the tendered costings could be negotiated and will often be asked to take a lead role in any such negotiations. Depending upon the advisory role of an engineer or architect the quantity surveyor may also be called upon to give more general advice, for example as to liquidated damages provision or even the most suitable form of contract. In a mirror image of these functions the quantity surveyor may be retained by a contractor in order to estimate the cost of works, price the bill of quantities, assist in the preparation of a tender and carry out negotiations. However, most substantial contractors employ their own quantity surveyors and it would be relatively unusual for quantity surveyors to be independently engaged except in respect of very substantial contracts. During the construction process, for works constructed under a traditional building contract, a quantity surveyor engaged by the employer will generally be required to assist the architect by advising the latter as to the value of work carried out for the purpose of providing interim and final payments and work to be carried out under proposed or actual variation instructions. Similarly a quantity surveyor engaged by the contractor will be required to measure work carried out by the contractor and work carried out by subcontractors. On projects constructed under design-and-build contracts the employer may not retain a quantity surveyor at all whereas on projects undertaken by management contractors the employer will generally retain a quantity surveyor to shadow the functions of the management contractor's quantity surveyor. Depending on the form of construction contract used, the role of the quantity surveyor may be prescribed in detail. At the completion of the works under a traditional construction contract a quantity surveyor engaged by the employer will generally be called upon to undertake a valuation of the contractor's final account. If the contractor has submitted a claim for loss and expense he will generally be required – in consultation with the employer's contract administrator – to advise the employer as to the value of that claim and to undertake such enquiries and negotiations as may be necessary. However, it should be kept in mind that quantity surveyors are increasingly being called upon to perform 'non-traditional' roles, for example as project managers (see Chapter 5) or in relation to particular contracts, for example drafting the client's brief in relation to design-and-build contracts. The RICS Schedule of Services, Categories 2 and 3, provide a useful indication of the range of services which quantity surveyors now offer.

In contrast to the role and functions of architects and engineers, the traditional scope of a quantity surveyor's duties to his client are relatively narrow. Whereas the architect or engineer is generally required to take decisions as to design, instructions to contractors or certification the traditional role of the quantity surveyor is generally confined to advising on matters of cost:

> All that a quantity surveyor can do is (a) to check that tenders of contractors or subcontractors are reasonably priced before he recommends acceptance; (b) to measure work executed accurately; (c) to exercise vigilance in the valuation of variations or the checking of the valuation of variations submitted to him by the contractor; (d) make a fair assessment of any additional sums which may be due to a contractor as a result of extension of time, acceleration instructions and so forth.[2]

It is this narrowness of function (and thus the limited consequences of a quantity surveyor carrying out his functions negligently) which partly explains why relatively few professional negligence actions are taken against quantity surveyors in comparison with architects and engineers. Moreover – as will be explained – even where the consequences of a quantity surveyor's error are potentially significant (for example a gross over valuation of work carried out), the employer will often have a remedy against the contractor under the terms of the contract which will mean that he suffers no loss. Of course once quantity surveyors step outside their traditional roles and begin to advise on issues beyond matters of cost and value, the risk that a negligent error will lead to a substantial claim increases. Thus quantity surveyors who take on the role of advisers on design or who carry out the functions of a contract administrator may run the same risks as architects or engineers carrying out those functions. In the field of claims consultancy – which is dominated by quantity surveyors – advice which extends beyond the issues of cost and value into the sphere of legal advice may result in quantity surveyors running the same risks as lawyers.[3]

---

2 Per Mr Recorder Jackson QC in *Burrell Hayward & Budd* v. *Chris Carnell and David Green* [unreported] 20 February 1992.
3 See Chapter 6.

Quantity surveyors' contracts

As with architects and engineers, there is no legal requirement that quantity surveyors enter into any particular form of contract. The normal rules of the law of contract will apply to any agreement between a quantity surveyor and his client. Thus although it is prudent for such agreements to be in writing, or at least evidenced by an exchange of correspondence, agreements are often oral or partially in writing and partially oral. Similarly, although it is prudent for all terms of a contract to be agreed before the commencement of services it is common practice for the substantial terms to be agreed at the outset and for remaining matters to be implied according to custom and practice or to be agreed subsequently. The RICS Form of Agreement follows a familiar structure, however, the following should be noted. The parties to the agreement are identified, as is the project. It is made clear that the Form of Agreement is to be read with the Form of Enquiry, Schedule of Services and Fee Offer which identify the work to be carried out and the payment to be made. (Quantity surveyors' fees are no longer fixed to a particular scale and their remuneration is entirely a matter for commercial negotiation between the parties.)[4] Condition 1.1 stipulates that the quantity surveyor will provide the services with reasonable care and skill. Condition 5 provides that he must carry professional indemnity insurance. Condition 11 provides for the use of a complaints procedure or adjudication in the event of a dispute, whilst Condition 12 provides for voluntary arbitration. Because of the narrow scope of his traditional functions it is usually less important for a quantity surveyor's contract of engagement to spell out his precise role and responsibilities. These will generally be clear. However, it is important to note that where the quantity surveyor performs a designated function under a construction contract, the terms of that contract may determine the scope of his duties. In particular quantity surveyors should be wary of provisions of the construction contract which may require the quantity surveyor to go beyond his usual tasks of valuation and the agreement of quantum and to empower him to make agreements as to liability.[5]

Just as it is open to an architect or engineer to provide warranties that his design will perform to a certain standard, so it is open to a quantity surveyor to provide warranties to the effect that a building can be built for a certain cost. Clearly such warranties will be rare and when employed should be used

---

4 In default of an agree sum or rate of remuneration, the courts will imply into the contract a term that a reasonable sum be paid. However, it should be noted that this will not necessarily be the same sum as would have been customary, but will be one which takes into account all aspects of the engagement – see *Gwyther* v. *Gaze* (1875) HBC (fourth edition) Vol II, p. 134.
5 See, for example, the facts of *John Laing Construction Ltd* v. *County & District Properties Ltd* 23 BLR 10 where it was unsuccessfully argued that a provision enabling the employer's quantity surveyor to agree amounts payable to the contractor clothed him with authority to agree an absolute entitlement to those amounts, as opposed to merely agreeing the quantum of any entitlement. Had the argument succeeded the quantity surveyor might have found himself in breach of his duties to the employer.

with great caution as the quantity surveyor is taking on the risk that, for reasons beyond his control, costs will rise. In the absence of such warranties the key obligation owed by a quantity surveyor to his client is the obligation to use reasonable skill and care. In the absence of an express term to that effect, the courts will imply such a term. As with architects and engineers, quantity surveyors' contracts occasionally contain obligations which purport to demand a higher degree of skill and care – for example the 'utmost' skill and care. Such obligations are very difficult, if not impossible, to distinguish from reasonable skill and care and generally speaking add little to that standard. As with all construction professionals, quantity surveyors are often required to provide warranties to third parties and it should be noted that the RICS provides a recommended form for these. The standard of care required by these warranties is almost always the same standard as is owed to the client under the contract.

Reasonable skill and care

As with other professionals the standard of reasonable skill and care is the standard to be expected of a reasonably competent quantity surveyor. In the absence of any reported examination of the particular standard appropriate to quantity surveyors the general principles set out by McNair J in the medical negligence case of *Bolam* v. *Friern Hospital Management Committee*[6] should be applied:

> Where you get a situation which involves the use of some special skill of competence . . . the test is the standard of the ordinary skilled man exercising and professing to have that special skill. A man need not possess the highest expert skill . . . it is sufficient if he exercises the ordinary skill of ordinary competent man exercising that particular art.

In particular, because the work of quantity surveyors involves a detailed knowledge of pricing techniques and the economic features of modern construction work, it is worth repeating the guidance provided by Bingham LJ in *Eckersly* v. *Binnie & Partners*:[7]

> A professional man should command the corpus of knowledge which forms part of the professional equipment of the ordinary member of his profession. He should not lag behind other ordinarily assiduous and intelligent members of his profession in knowledge of new advances, discoveries and developments in his field. He should be alert to the

---

6 [1957] 1 WLR 582 at 586.
7 (1988) 18 Con LR 1.

hazards and risks inherent in any professional task he undertakes to the extent that other ordinarily competent members of the profession would be alert. He must bring to any professional task he undertakes no less expertise, skill and care than other ordinarily competent members would bring but need bring no more. The law does not require of a professional man that he be a paragon combining the qualities of polymath and prophet.

As with architects and engineers, the fact that a quantity surveyor is relatively junior or inexperienced will not of itself provide a defence to being judged by the standards of the ordinarily competent member of his profession.[8] By the same token a very highly qualified and highly experienced quantity surveyor is not to be judged more harshly because of his ability and experience. In practice the courts may make some allowance in respect of the standard which the employer could reasonably expect to believe he was getting. Consequently they are more likely to be forgiving of mistakes which lie on the borderline of negligence and mere errors of judgment where the employer has knowingly employed an inexperienced quantity surveyor than they would be where the professional has held himself out to be highly experienced.

Examples

Costs estimates and bills of quantities

A quantity surveyor may be asked by an employer to provide cost estimates, either of carrying out the whole project or part of the project, based on the architect or engineer's design. The employer may rely upon these estimates to decide whether or not to proceed with works or whether to proceed with one of several options. Depending on the nature of the works the employer may also rely upon the estimates in order to anticipate the cash flow requirements of the project. A negligent error on the part of he quantity surveyor may thus cause the employer loss. If the employer finds that having tendered the works he is unable to afford any of the returned tenders because the quantity surveyor has underestimated the price, he may be forced to abandon the project altogether. On a cost-plus contract he may end up paying the contractor far more than he had anticipated – or possibly can afford. In the relatively unusual circumstances where the quantity surveyor is employed by a contractor an underestimate of the costs may lead to the contractor entering into a contract which will lead him to suffer a loss.

---

8 See by analogy *Cardy* v. *Taylor* (1994) 38 Con LR 79 where an unqualified person holding himself out as practising as an architect was judged by the standards of a reasonably competent architect.

Bills of quantities are prepared by a quantity surveyor using standard methods of measurement with which he is expected to be familiar. As a contractual device, although widely used, they have attracted criticism because of the risks they pose to employers by reason of:

> the opportunities they offer, in conjunction with the standard methods, for securing pricing advantages, because over- or under-estimates (or failures to comply with the standard methods) which can be detected in the bills at the tender stage, and variations of the work which are already known to be probable at that time, can be anticipated by the appropriate weighting of the tender prices so as to present the owner with an apparently attractive overall price which in reality will need to be adjusted upwards on re-measurement, while undetected errors will in any event be adjusted.[9]

In assessing the cost of works a quantity surveyor must have regard not merely to the current state of prices and materials but also as to the likely trends in both. Where there are significant uncertainties he should indicate this to the client. Of course as in any sphere of professional activity the estimation of likely costs is a matter of professional judgment and the mere fact that actual costs turned out to higher or lower is not of itself evidence of negligence. In *Copthorne Hotel (Newcastle) Ltd* v. *Arup Associates*[10] piling costs had been estimated at £425,000 whereas they in fact turned out to be £975,000. No evidence was given as to how the estimation had come to be so far removed from the actual total and the court held that the mere fact of this discrepancy was not enough to establish negligence: although negligence was one possibility, there were others, including over-specification or a change in market conditions, and in order to find a breach of duty the court had to be satisfied that these were not the causes of the discrepancy. By contrast, errors in the preparation of bills of quantities are likely to be more mundane and for the most part are processing errors – additions or subtractions being incorrect, parts of the specification omitted or double-counted. Whilst there are older authorities which suggest that such errors may occur and not necessarily be negligent,[11] it is doubtful whether such an approach would be followed today, and as a general rule an error in a bill of quantities can be said to be *prima facie* evidence of negligence without the need for further proof of lack of reasonable care. Of course if the error is truly one of judgment, there is room for a defence that reasonable care has

---

9 *Hudson's Building and Engineering Contracts*, eleventh edition, para. 2.226.
10 (1996) 58 Con LR 105.
11 See *London School Board* v. *Northcroft, Southern Neighbour*, cited in *Hudson's Building Contracts* (fourth edition) Vol II, p. 147, where on a project to a value of £12,000 quantity surveyors were held not to be liable for errors of £118 and £12 because they had employed a competent skilled clerk who had carried out hundreds of intricate calculations correctly.

been employed even though the wrong result has been obtained. Thus when assessing whether quantities are sufficient rather than excessive there may be an element of judgment and room for disagreement.

Advice upon tender

After tenders have been received the quantity surveyor will draw up comparisons and will advise the employer (either directly or through the architect of engineer). In most larger projects the quantity surveyor will then be part of the employer's team for the purposes of negotiating with shortlisted contractors so that the employer can obtain the best price. Often the contractor's priced bill of quantities will form the basis of negotiation, particularly if the contractor has been asked to price for different options or is asked to look for savings in particular areas. When examining the contractor's proposals the quantity surveyor should take care not to accept rates which are unreasonable or unclear in a way which may later enable the contractor to exploit the lack of clarity. In *Tyrer* v. *District Auditor of Monmouthshire*[12] a quantity surveyor was found to have acted in breach of duty for approving excessive quantities and prices with builders not just because of arithmetical miscalculations but because he should have appreciated that the quantities and rates were excessive. Where the contractor's priced bill of quantities contains an obvious error which is against the contractor's interests it has been suggested that the quantity surveyor is not merely obliged to report this fact to his employer but also is under a moral obligation to report the matter to the contractor.[13] The more prudent course is probably to report the error to the employer with a strong recommendation that if he is minded not to notify the contractor of his error he should take legal advice.[14]

Administering the contract

It is unlikely that a quantity surveyor would be required to carry out the functions traditionally accorded to an architect or engineer of giving instructions, inspecting work the quality of work and issuing certificates. Rather his role is likely to be assisting the architect or engineer by carrying out valuations for the purposes of interim payments or variation instructions and latterly valuing the contractor's claims for loss and expense. However, depending on the form of construction contract employed his duties may extend beyond these roles and in any event he is likely to be called upon by the employer to

---

12 [1973] 23.
13 *Dutton* v. *Louth Corporation* (1955) 116 EG 128.
14 A contract may be avoided if one party knowingly takes advantage of an obvious mistake by the other. The NJCC Code of Procedure for Single Stage Selective Tendering (1996) provides that where errors are found the tenderer should be given an opportunity of confirming, withdrawing or amending his tender.

provide advice as to the overall and projected expenditure and cash flows. Moreover on very small contracts the quantity surveyor may find himself engaged as contract administrator in lieu of an architect or engineer. In such circumstances his duty remains that he will exercise the reasonable care and skill to be exercised by a reasonably competent quantity surveyor except where he has purported to exercise a skill which is plainly outside his profession (for example, providing advice on design) when he may well be judged according to the standard of the professional whose work he has undertaken. In relation to his valuation functions it is important to keep in mind that, unless he is required to do so by the terms of his contract, a quantity surveyor is not obliged to monitor the progress of the works or give general advice to the employer. These are the responsibilities of the architect or engineer. In *Aubrey Jacobus & Partners* v. *Gerrard*[15] HH Judge Stabb QC said:

> It is suggested that the quantity surveyor was under a duty to monitor or control the costs and advise the client. I am satisfied that no such duty exists. The architect is the team leader: he is primarily responsible for design and the cost of it. If called upon, the quantity surveyor is there to provide information as to cost but not in my view to monitor or control it by carrying out checks at regular intervals as was suggested.

Valuations and post-completion works

Most construction contracts require interim valuations to be made, usually at monthly intervals, the amount certified being the amount of work executed as well as the value of unfixed goods and materials on site (and sometimes off site). Although these are interim valuations and can be corrected, a quantity surveyor none the less owes the employer a duty to take reasonable care. Overvaluation on interim certificates can lead to difficulties for the employer if the contractor becomes insolvent or if the sum certified is so greatly in excess of the value of the work done that there is insufficient money to withhold from the contractor on later certificates to make good the over-payment. Generally the quantity surveyor will discharge his obligations by a cursory examination of the site – it being accepted that the valuation is an approximate one. However, four points ought to be noted.

1   The quantity surveyor should try to carry out a fair valuation even if he has no contractual status under the main construction contract and is simply acting as the agent of the employer. Any bias or lack of fairness in the valuations may damage the employer's legal position in the event of a substantive dispute with the contractor.

15 [1981] unreported.

2   As noted above, more care should be taken in respect of later valuations because of the reduced scope for correcting any overpayment.

3   Particular care ought to be taken where the quantity surveyor has reason to believe that the contractor may be attempting to misrepresent the amount of work executed.

4   A quantity surveyor is required to measure the work carried out. It is no part of his function to assess whether that work has been carried out well or badly and he is under no duty to report defects. That said, if substantially defective work comes to the attention of the quantity surveyor and he has reason to believe that it has not come to the attention of the employer's architect, he may owe the employer an obligation to alert the architect to the defects.

Following practical completion a quantity surveyor is usually required to undertake the valuation of the final account for measured work and variations and the valuation of any loss and expense claims (or other permissible claims) submitted by the contractor. Unlike interim valuations this exercise clearly requires precision and unsurprisingly most forms of contract provide for the contractor to submit full information to the employer and for the latter to have a considerable period thereafter (for example three months) in which to prepare the final account. The quantity surveyor is usually charged with obtaining all such further information as he may require from the contractor and to this end it is quite common for quantity surveyors engaged by the employer to make repeated requests for information from contractors. Similarly the valuation of variations probably requires more careful scrutiny that interim valuations because they too are generally not susceptible of correction. Whilst the existing rates are usually employed, the quantity surveyor may none the less be faced with a difficult exercise, not least because the architect may also require to be advised as to the loss and expense consequences of a particular period of delay. In respect of larger contracts substantial variations may be negotiated with quantity surveyors from both parties advising their clients as to the cost consequences of particular aspects of the proposed instruction.

Duties to third parties

There are not many recorded professional negligence disputes involving quantity surveyors and where they occur they usually concern the performance of contractual duties. However, it is quite possible that persons who have no contractual relationship with a quantity surveyor might wish to consider taking action against him. Whether and to what extent such actions can succeed will depend upon whether they can make out the existence of an actionable duty of care in tort (see Chapter 1) or bring themselves within the class of persons who have a right of action under statute. In either case such actions are uncommon and may be best discussed by reference to examples. However, where a duty of care (or similar statutory duty) is found to exist, the test for breach of duty is exactly the same: did the quantity surveyor act with the skill and care to be expected of a reasonably competent member of his profession?

Persons who act in reliance on a representation

There may be situations where, although there is no contractual relationship, something said or done by a quantity surveyor causes a person to act in such a way that he suffers loss. An example might be a situation where, prior to there being any contract, the quantity surveyor volunteers an opinion to a prospective client as to how much a piece of work is likely to cost. If the prospective client then relies upon that estimate and the estimate turns out to have been made negligently then even if there is no contractual relationship (for example because the prospective client decides to do without the services of a quantity surveyor) he may pursue the quantity surveyor for losses which he suffers as a result of that reliance.

Contractors

It would be very unusual for a contractor to wish to take action against a quantity surveyor engaged by the employer. Unlike architects or engineers they do not have a certification role and will often merely advise the architect. However, it is possible that where the quantity surveyor has negligently undervalued the work completed and the employer has become insolvent a contractor might contend that he was owed a duty of care. It is very doubtful whether such an action could succeed, given the state of the law concerning similar actions against architects.[16]

Purchasers of defective dwelling houses

Under the Defective Premises Act 1972 (see Chapter 1) a quantity surveyor who inspects the construction of a dwelling house owes a subsequent purchaser a duty to see that it is constructed in a workmanlike manner, with proper materials and so that it is fit for habitation when completed.[17] If he is in breach of that duty the subsequent purchaser may sue the quantity surveyor. However, the value of this right of action to any subsequent purchaser is limited. In the first place the right exists only in respect of a dwelling house – that is, a house or a flat intended for human habitation. Secondly it is likely that in order to succeed the purchaser must show that property was rendered 'unfit for habitation'. Lastly under the Limitation Act 1980 the right

---

16 See *Pacific Associates Inc* v. *Baxter* [1990] 1 QB 193.
17 The Act applies to all construction professionals.

to recover damages ceases six years from the date of completion of the dwelling.

Persons who are sued for losses also caused by the quantity surveyor

Contribution proceedings against quantity surveyors are not unheard of. For example an employer will sue his architect for over-certification. The architect will then take contribution proceedings against the quantity surveyor, alleging that his certificates were based on the latter's valuations, which were made negligently.

Practical considerations in claims against quantity surveyors

Reference should be made to Chapter 7 for a full discussion of the practicalities of professional negligence actions against construction professionals. However, in respect of quantity surveyors the following facts and matters should be kept in mind.

1   *Proving breach of duty.* In almost every instance it will be necessary for the person who proposes taking action against a quantity surveyor to obtain an expert opinion from someone qualified and practising in that profession. This opinion will generally be required before proceedings are commenced. A professional defending such proceedings will generally also require an expert opinion.
2   *Insurance.* The adequacy of the professional's indemnity cover will often be a material consideration All practising quantity surveyors should carry professional indemnity insurance. Moreover under the RICS 1992 Form of Agreement the liability of a quantity surveyor is expressly stated to be limited to the limit of cover provided by that insurance.
3   *Adjudication.* Although it is unusual for a claim against a quantity surveyor to be referred to adjudication, this could happen. The RICS Form of Agreement 1992 makes provision for it and sets out the adjudication rules. A reference would be made by the quantity surveyor seeking payment of his fees or by a client who seeks to take a tactical advantage by employing this remedy.
4   *Arbitration.* A quantity surveyor could insert a condition into his contract of engagement for any dispute arising between himself and the employer to be referred to arbitration. The RICS 1992 Form of Agreement provides the option of going to arbitration. However, if a different form of contract is in use care should be taken to check whether there is a compulsory arbitration clause.
5   *Limitation periods.* Like all construction professionals, quantity suveyors owe their employers a tortious duty of care which is usually the mirror

image of the contractual duty of care. Employers may seek to rely upon the tortious duty in situations where, because more than six years has elapsed between the breach of duty and the commencement of proceedings, the claim in contract would be barred by the operation of Section 5 of the Limitation Act 1980 but the employer can none the less show that damage was first suffered within time or can rely upon Section 14A of that Act (see Chapter 1).

5 Project managers

Project managers are a relatively new breed of construction professional whose origin probably results from the increased complexity of construction projects and the specialisation of the various parties working within those projects: there are now so many parties engaged in such a complex web of activities that the client requires an additional professional to co-ordinate and keep watch over them.

The functions of a project manager

There is no recognised definition of a project manager and the best indication of the nature of the tasks commonly undertaken by him is to be found in the guidance provided by the various professional bodies. One of the longest-established sets of such guidance was the RICS 1988 Guidance Notes for 'Project Management: Construction Monitoring'[1] which set out at length the typical functions of a project manager, which it contrasted with the more restrictive requirements of construction monitoring. Project management tasks were listed as:

1 *Client's requirements.* Discussing the client's requirements which will be concerned with space, function, operation, quality, timing, costs, including life cycling costs.
2 *Establishment of project team.* The initial analysis of the client's requirements will determine who should comprise the principal members of the team. The team may be expanded as the project evolves. The project manager's functions may include selection, recommendation, appointment, agreement of fees and development of systems of communication between project team members.
3 *Development of programme for implementation.* The programme to include stages for agreement of concept and detail design development,

---

1 Now superseded by the Guidance Notes attached to the RICS Project Management Agreement and Conditions of Engagement.

ıning and other statutory requirements, pre-construction and post-
struction activities.

ıblishment of a budget. Establishing a budget covering all elements
ıncluding fees, construction costs, etc.

5 *Construction economics.* Arranging where agreed for capital and life
cycle costs studies on different forms of construction, use of materials
and design.

6 *Legal services.* Liaising with the client's solicitor on matters relating to
the development.

7 *Tendering and contractual arrangements.* Arranging for selection of contractors, advising on tendering methods, forms of contract. Presentation
of reports and evaluation of tenders, together with recommendations for
negotiation prior to the award of a contract, where appropriate.

8 *Cash flow.* Preparing regular cash flow forecasts and statements.
Authorising payments due under building contracts, consultants' fees
and other outgoings.

9 *Review of programme.* Using reasonable endeavours to keep the project
on programme and in line with the client's expectations. Bringing the
client's attention to significant deviations from programme, explaining
causes and making recommendations for corrective action.

10 *Project procedures.* Establishing a management framework within which
the project team, including contractors, can function, including setting
up regular meetings, procedures for the issue of instructions and their
approval, preparation and circulation of minutes.

11 *Control of construction works during contract stage.* Co-ordinating
or appointing suitable organisation to control and co-ordinate the work
on site. Establishing clear lines of responsibility or all on site personnel
and establishing working relationships between the design team and
contractors.

12 *Monitoring performance and progress.* Monitoring work in progress,
costs and the performance of the professional team.

13 *Quality control.* Setting up methods for inspection of standards of
workmanship and materials and compliance with drawings and specification, or alternatively, arranging third party insurance for Quality
Assurance schemes. Ensure that any warranties and guarantees obtained
have the client's interests endorsed.

14 *Financial settlement.* Reviewing all payments made or due under all building contracts, consultant fee arrangements and the finance agreement.

15 *Commissioning/hand-over.* Arranging the hand-over of the building after
operational testing and full commissioning of all services. Arranging for
maintenance manuals, test certificates and guarantees to be passed to the
client, together with 'as built' drawings and 'as instructed' diagrams for
services, etc.

16 *Post-construction management duties.* Providing where agreed all
necessary co-ordination duties in connection with the client's relocation

proposals including, if required, the organisation of fitting out works using techniques similar to that employed on the main project. Maintaining contract during the defects liability period and ensuring that all defects are dealt with satisfactorily.

The above list of functions serves to illustrate the range of tasks which can be undertaken by a project manager. However, it should be noted that in all cases it is for the client and the professional to decide which tasks he should undertake, and it is very common to find bespoke contracts whereby architects or quantity surveyors have their responsibilities tied in to the particular needs of the project. On larger projects the focus of the project manager's activities will be upon co-ordination and acting as the interface between the other professionals and the client. His day-to-day monitoring of the works may be restricted or relatively unimportant, these being the tasks of the architect and the quantity surveyor, who report to him. On smaller projects he may supervise the operation of the contract itself, dealing directly with the contractor and carrying out a general Clerk of Works role.

A project manager's contract

The project manager may be appointed in his capacity as an architect, engineer or quantity surveyor to carry out project management services under the terms of one of the standard form of contracts provided by professional bodies such as the RICS. However, it is very common, particularly in respect of larger developments, for project managers' contracts of appointment to be bespoke. In such situations the contract will generally take the following form. The identities of the parties will be set out together with a reference to the project to which the appointment relates. The services which the project manager is required to provide in respect of that project will be listed – usually in an appendix. These services will include a level of monitoring of the progress of the works, co-ordination of the professional team, ensuring adequate channels of communication, acting as the employer's representative in respect of all matters concerning the professional team and (depending on the contract and if not covered by the architect or quantity surveyor) carrying out the same role with the contractor, carrying out certain liaison tasks with statutory bodies, letting agents and other third parties, acting as the client's eyes and ears in relation to the project and advising the client generally at all stages. Occasionally the terms will include provisions such as 'procuring' that the project is constructed in accordance with the client's requirements, although it is doubtful whether this means anything more than using reasonable skill and care to see that the other professionals and the building contractor carry out their obligations.

Reasonable skill and care

As with all construction professionals, the primary obligations which he owes to his client are to be found in the express or implied terms of his contract. Most contracts will not only set out the range of services which he is to perform but will indicate the standard of performance, which is almost always to employ reasonable skill and care. Because there is, as yet, no recognition of a distinct profession of project managers it is likely that when ascertaining the relevant duty of skill and care the court will look to the profession from which the project manager comes. Thus if a quantity surveyor is the project manager the standard will be the standard of skill and care to be expected of a reasonably competent quantity surveyor holding himself out as carrying on project management work. If the project manager is an architect the standard will be that of the reasonably competent architect holding himself out as carrying on project management work. If, as is sometimes the case, the project manager is a multidisciplinary firm, possessing the skills or architects and surveyors, the standard of care may be fixed accordingly.

Because the project manager's role is concerned largely with supervision and co-ordination most professional negligence actions against project managers involve an allegation that the project manager failed to control particular aspects of the costs, failed to ensure that other construction professionals had access to correct information or failed to prevent another construction professional from making an important error. Thus in *Chesham Properties Ltd* v. *Bucknall Austin Project Management Services Ltd*[2] the claimant sued both the architect and the project manager in respect of what it alleged were excessive extensions of time together with loss and expense awarded to the contractor. The court found that where it would have been apparent to a reasonably competent project manager that the architect was not performing his duty he had an obligation to inform the claimant. However, in *Royal Brompton Hospital NHS Trust* v. *Hammond and others* (No. 7)[3] where the claimant made the same complaint the judge found that it was no part of the project manager's duty to second-guess the decisions of the architect:

> While each case depends upon its own facts and the particular contractual arrangements which the parties have made, it is, I think, plain . . . that in the ordinary way a professional person who is engaged to provide a service for a client for whom other professionals are also providing services is entitled to proceed on the basis that the other professionals will properly perform the services which they have undertaken to perform.[4]

2 (1996) 82 BLR 92.
3 76 Con LR 148.
4 At 180.

Whilst there are few reported cases involving project managers it is probably worth noting that claims against them are likely to be ancillary to claims against other professionals. In the two cases mentioned above, the claims against the project managers were ancillary to the claims against the architects for negligence over certification. In claims involving some design problem the claim against the project manager is likely to concern his alleged failure to provide the design professionals with all relevant information. However, those professionals are also likely to be the subject of the same proceedings on the basis that notwithstanding the involvement of a project manager it was their responsibility to obtain the relevant information. In claims involving cost overruns it is not inconceivable that all the professional team will be the subject of legal proceedings, including the project manager, on the basis that they all contributed to the additional and avoidable expense by individual errors, delays and failure to co-ordinate with each other. When considering how much of any loss should be borne by a project manager who failed to act with reasonable skill and care the court will have regard to the extent to which poor management was really the cause of the problem.

Practical considerations in claims against project managers

Reference should be made to Chapter 7 for a full discussion of the practicalities of professional negligence actions against project managers. However, in respect of quantity surveyors the following facts and matters should be kept in mind.

1   *Form of contract.* Typically the project manager will be an architect, engineer or quantity surveyor employed to undertake project management services. Whilst he may be working to a bespoke appointment, it is equally possible that he may be working to one of the standard forms of agreement produced by the professional bodies. In the latter instance the practical considerations are likely to be as for those professionals (see Chapters 3 and 4).
2   *Proving breach of duty.* In almost every instance it will be necessary for the person who proposes taking action against a project manager to obtain an expert opinion from someone qualified and practising in that profession. If the project manager is an architect the expert should be an architect carrying on project management work. This opinion will generally be required before proceedings are commenced. A professional defending such proceedings will generally also require an expert opinion.
3   *Insurance.* The adequacy of the professional's indemnity cover will often be a material consideration. Because the project manager is almost always an architect, engineer or quantity surveyor he will be required to carry professional indemnity insurance by the rules of his professional association if not under the contract itself. However, most

bespoke contracts will provide for a certain level of professional indemnity insurance to be carried.

4   *Adjudication.* Even if he is not appointed on a standard form contract, the project manager is likely to be working to a contract that expressly or impliedly imparts the right of either party to go to adjudication. Because of the specialised nature of a project manager's services and the usual involvement of some other party, adjudication is probably an undesirable route to resolving disputes. None the less it may be adopted.

5   *Arbitration.* Again if the project manager is working to one of the standard forms of contract it is quite possible there will be a provision at least providing the possibility for any dispute arising between himself and the employer to be referred to arbitration. It is unlikely that a bespoke contract will contain a compulsory arbitration clause because of the obvious disadvantages of being unable to bring other parties into the dispute (see Chapter 7).

6   *Limitation periods.* As with all construction professionals, project managers owe their employers a tortious duty of care which is usually the mirror image of the contractual duty of care. Employers may seek to rely upon the tortious duty in situations where, because more than six years has elapsed between the breach of duty and the commencement of proceedings, the claim in contract would be barred by the operation of Section 5 of the Limitation Act 1980 but the employer can none the less show that damage was first suffered within time or can rely upon Section 14A of that Act (see Chapter 1).

6   Claims consultants and expert witnesses

One of the unintended consequences of the increasing sophistication of construction contracts has been the increased dependence of employers and contractors upon professionals providing advice in relation to the intricacies of contracts and advice and related services in relation to claims. To a lesser extent this dependence appears in relation to very substantial projects where bespoke contracts are employed and/or there is a complex web of legal relations. Here lawyers acting for both the employer and the contractor are often part of the pre-contract teams. More generally the dependence is exhibited by the use of claims consultants, lawyers and experts to advise and act in respect of contractual claims and the legal processes of conciliation, adjudication, arbitration and litigation. Certainly in relation to larger projects claims consultants, if not lawyers, can be seen to be an integral part of the professional team along with architects, engineers and quantity surveyors.

Claims consultants and their obligations

Claims consultants evolved as a consequence of the ever more complex requirements of contractors claims under the main forms of construction contracts and the very substantial sums involved. In particular, claims for extensions of time giving rise to loss and expense in respect of large construction projects have developed into an art form requiring not merely the use of sophisticated programming techniques, but the marshalling of extensive information often held in banks of files in support of a range of different financial costs. As most of these claims were traditionally put together by quantity surveyors, the 1970s and early 1980s saw quantity surveyors specialising in this type of work setting themselves up as independent claims consultants and that profession still dominates the make-up of most claims consultancies. However, the larger firms of claims consultants will now number architects and engineers amongst their number (if not also lawyers) in order to offer a range of professional services to employers and contractors. Claims consultants now advise from the inception of a project until the final resolution of outstanding disputes. In addition they will represent clients in adjudications and arbitrations and some even offer the services of expert witnesses. Whilst there is no recognised professional body representing claims consultants (although the employees may belong to representative bodies appropriate to their qualifications) it has been forcefully contended that they are none the less a separate 'profession'[1] and just as project managers are beginning to be considered as distinct professionals by the courts so claims consultants will probably recognise the profession of claims consultants.[2]

However, what is the duty owed by a claims consultant to his client? There are two possibilities. The more obvious answer is that the standard of care to be performed by a claims consultant is the standard to be expected of a reasonably competent member of his profession. In this way a claims consultant is treated in the same way as any other professional and judged according to the *Bolam* test which underlies professional negligence for all professions. However, this formulation suffers from the disadvantage that the 'profession' is relatively new and that the scope of its functions ranges across tasks traditionally undertaken by other professionals. Thus where a claims consultant is charged with putting together a claim on the basis of available material he may be doing the same work which would be undertaken by a surveyor in direct employment or engaged specifically for that purpose. In contrast the claims consultant may represent a client at an arbitration hearing, having drafted the pleadings, collated the evidence and advised the client as to the merits. In so doing he is carrying out the same functions as a solicitor. Arguably, therefore, it may be more appropriate for a claims consultant's duty of care to be defined by reference not to the novel profession of 'claims consultant' but rather to the standard of care to be performed by the professional in whose traditional field he is practising.[3] This approach works well in situations where the client's contract is with one of the larger firms of claims consultants, which employs a raft of professionals including architects, quantity surveyors and lawyers. It is also consistent with the well established rule that within one profession there is no distinction between the experienced professional and the novice.

This approach may be difficult to justify in practice. What of the situation where the client engages a one-man-band claims consultant knowing that the latter is qualified solely as a quantity surveyor who, whilst he has some experience in legal matters, does not hold himself out as an expert? It seems wrong in principle that that person should necessarily be judged by the standards of, say, a reasonably competent solicitor. Moreover many of the functions

---

1 See Neil F. Jones, *Professional Negligence in the Construction Industry* (1998), at p. 146.
2 The presence of claims consultants – if not their separate professional status – has been judicially commented upon for some time; see for example *McAlpine Humberoak* v. *McDermott International* (1992) 58 BLR 1.
3 This formulation receives support in *Professional Negligence in the Construction Industry* at pp. 147 and 148.

undertaken by a claims consultant do not fall neatly into 'quantity surveyor's work' or 'solicitors' work' but may straddle the boundary between the two and may additionally involve the provision of commercial or tactical advice. The answer is probably that the court will follow the traditional path of judging a defendant by the standards of the 'reasonably competent claims consultant.' However, that standard will in part be fixed by reference to the task undertaken and the standard expected of the profession traditionally practising in that area. Thus if a legally qualified claims consultant fails to apply standard methods of measurement to quantities, thereby understating his contractor client's entitlement, he is likely to be judged in relation to that failing according to the standard to be expected of a reasonably competent surveyor, unless he has expressly warned his client that he does not have that level of expertise. Similarly the quantity surveyor claims consultant who undertakes to represent his client at an arbitration is likely to be judged on that matter according to the standard of the reasonably competent solicitor, unless he has unequivocally made the client aware of the limitations of his experience. Where such warnings have been provided the court is still likely to find that the standard of care is sufficiently high that obvious mistakes should not occur. In an alleged breach of duty which involves no particular recognised field of expertise – for example the provision of commercial advice – the court will still apply the test of the reasonably competent claims consultant, but will have no readily available body of expertise to judge that standard by. It follows that to the extent that a claims consultant holds himself out as a jack of all trades the court will judge him as a master of all of them, unless he has warned the client that this is not the case.

It is worth noting the particular areas where claims consultants may be likely to perform in such as way as to be in breach of duty to their clients.

Pre-contract advice

It is not unknown for claims consultants to be engaged to advise on particular aspects of an intended contract, although this function is usually confined to solicitors. Without an express disclaimer (which might well make the advice worthless to the client) there is a substantial risk that a claims consultant undertaking this kind of work will be judged by the standards of a reasonably competent solicitor. Moreover the courts traditionally allow very little room for error in the interpretation of contractual clauses, particularly if they have obviously onerous consequences for the client. By the same token claims consultants who are asked to consider a proposed contract in general terms should pay particular care to the risk of hidden dangers in the form of exclusions of rights, limitation of rights, the imposition of additional burdens (for example novations of other contracts and incorporation of main contractors' terms into subcontracts) and difficult conditions precedent. In detecting and advising upon these clauses the claims consultant is likely to be judged according to the standards of a reasonably competent solicitor. Moreover if called upon to give commercial advice in respect of the overall contract the claims consultant must be extremely careful to ensure that he has all the necessary information to hand and that he correctly identifies the variables, uncertainties and assumptions upon which his advice is provided.

Advice during the contract

Claims consultants may be asked to advise during the currency of a contract, usually in one or more of three circumstances. As identified above, they may be asked to advise upon the operation of a particular term. Secondly, and more usually at this stage, they may be asked to advise upon a particularly difficult potential claim which has arisen. Lastly, they may be asked to provide on-going advice with a view to protecting the employer or the contractor in anticipated legal proceedings which may follow the completion of the contract. It is quite common for claims consultants to be fully engaged at an early stage on large projects when it becomes clear that there will be some substantial dispute to be resolved at the end concerning extensions of time, loss and expense or both. The three different potential sets of circumstances illustrate the range of skills which a claims consultant may be called upon to exhibit. As to the first, he is required to provide competent legal advice, which may extend to advising the client that he should retain a solicitor or even counsel. As to the second he is also required to gather and marshal material so that an effective claim can be made. As to the third, the claims consultant may be advising the client as to how he should best prepare for any eventual proceedings and how he should deal with the employer or contractor (as the case may be) in the interim. He may be involved in drafting correspondence which sets out to record his client's position or he may advise on a certain course of action – for example the compromise of certain rights. In exercising all of the first and third of these skills the claims consultant may be required to perform to a standard of care appropriate to a lawyer knowledgeable in construction matters, or at least a non-lawyer experienced in such disputes and fully aware of his obligation to inform his clients if the job in hand is beyond his competence. In the gathering of evidence the standard of care is more difficult to judge – this not being a task where the skills of a lawyer are necessarily required – and it is likely that the court would devise some hybrid standard of care appropriate to someone holding himself out as competent to do that kind of work.

Advice during legal proceedings

Occasionally claims consultants act for their clients in relation to legal proceedings in place of lawyers (usually adjudications and occasionally arbitrations – see below). In so doing, unless there is an express term in their agreement to the contrary, they are likely to be required to perform to the standard of care to be expected of lawyers experienced in those fields. However, in the usual case (and particular in larger cases) claims consultants would hand over to lawyers at this stage, albeit that they may still be retained to assist the lawyers in the gathering and presentation of evidence. In so doing, whilst they will not be expected to act with the degree of skill and care expected of lawyers, they will be expected to act with the level of reasonable competence to be expected of someone holding himself out as competent to sift and weigh potential evidence and play an important role in its presentation.

Expert witnesses and their obligations

When considering the liabilities of expert witnesses it is first necessary to appreciate the role that they are required to play. All construction professionals are 'experts' in the sense that their expertise is required by the client, who may then rely upon their advice. When the client is in dispute with a construction professional he may retain another professional in the same discipline to advise him as to the nature of the problem which he faces and how to get round it. For example, where an employer is in dispute with his architect as to whether a particular design which appears to be defective can be made to work, the employer may appoint a further architect to provide him with independent advice on the design. That further architect is not an 'expert witness' in the sense employed in this chapter. He is merely a further architect with similar obligations to exercise reasonable skill and care as were owed by the first architect. An 'expert witness' is someone whose expertise has been sought so that he may provide evidence on behalf of the client in legal proceedings. He owes slightly different duties to those generally owed by construction professionals to their clients and benefits from the substantial protection of immunity from suit – that is, he cannot be sued – in respect of certain functions which he undertakes.

As indicated in Chapter 1, in the vast majority of cases the court reaches its decision as to whether a professional acted with reasonable skill and care assisted by the evidence of other professionals who provide an opinion as to what the ordinarily skilled member of the profession would have done in the relevant circumstances. Whilst the ultimate decision as to whether a particular act or omission is for the court, the court is not usually permitted to make findings as to what constitutes the standard without basing those findings on expert evidence. However, because that evidence is necessary to enable the courts to make the findings, the courts have approached the requirements for experts rigorously. In the first place the expert who is to give evidence must be suitably qualified. An architect is unlikely to be able to give suitably qualified evidence in a case concerning the reasonable standard of care to be exercised by an engineer. Indeed a non-practising engineer may find that his ability to provide evidence in respect of the standard of care demanded from a practising engineer is put in doubt. In *Sansom* v. *Metcalfe*

Hambleton & Co.[4] a building surveyor failed to draw his client's attention to a crack in a wall which, it was alleged, indicated structural defects. The judge at first instance preferred the claimant's evidence that this was negligent over the defendant's evidence that it was not, even though the claimant's evidence was given by a structural engineer and the defendant's evidence was given by a building surveyor. The Court of Appeal held that this finding could not stand. Butler-Sloss LJ said:

> A court should be slow to find a professionally qualified man guilty of a breach of his duty of skill and care towards a client (or third party) without evidence from those within the same profession as to the standard expected on the facts of the case and the failure of the professionally qualified man to measure up to that standard.

Secondly the expert witness must have confined his evidence to matters which are properly before him and upon which he is entitled to comment. In particular he should not stray outside his area of expertise to comment on matters of law or matters within the expertise of other disciplines. He should ensure that he has mastered all the relevant facts and has not proceeded on the basis of a misunderstanding of the facts or unjustified assumptions. Indeed in order to enable the court better to assess the soundness of an expert's approach to a particular issue it is a requirement that he should provide in his report the substance of his instructions and indicate where appropriate the documentary material upon which he has based his opinion. Legal proceedings concerning construction professionals often involve very substantial quantities of documentation and one of the tasks expected of an expert is that he will master this documentation so as to enable him to provide a balanced and thorough opinion.

The expert must understand the nature of the function he is required to address. He is to provide evidence of technical matters and the standards adopted in his profession. He is not required to provide an opinion as to what he personally would have done. In *Royal Brompton NHS Trust* v. *Hammond (No. 7)*[5] HH Judge Richard Seymour QC emphasised the importance of the expert appreciating the distinction between his own standards and those of the profession.

> It is, in my judgment, essential for an expert witness in the trial of a professional negligence action to perform what is actually a very difficult task, at least unless one is experienced in doing it, and that is to put to one side his own professional standards and to concentrate on the standards of the ordinarily competent member of his profession. There is a

4 [1998] PNLR 542.
5 76 Con LR 148 at 166.

natural temptation to regard one's own standards as those which should be shared by all members of one's profession, but as those who are approached to act as expert witnesses are often approached just because they are especially prominent members of their profession or particularly experienced, it is a temptation which must be resisted.

Last, and most important, an expert is required to serve two masters. He is instructed by his client and must carry out those instructions to the best of his ability, but he is also instructed by the court and must prepare his reports and give his evidence as an impartial expert. Indeed his overriding duty is to the court and where appropriate this duty may require him not to follow his client's instructions. The rules of court prescribe that an expert must sign an expert's declaration stating amongst other things that he has understood and fulfilled his duty to the court, that he has not been persuaded to provide a professional opinion with which he does not agree and that where there are different views as to what might be appropriate in a particular situation he has expressed the range of those views.[6] Failure by an expert to comply with these obligations may lead to his evidence being debarred before any proceedings take place.[7] More often it will lead to the court attaching little or no weight to the evidence he provides.[8]

Because of the importance attached to the impartiality of experts' evidence the courts have been reluctant to permit experts' clients suing their experts in respect of the way in which they give their evidence in court. The justification for this protection – which takes the form of immunity from proceedings – is that experts should not feel constrained by their client's best interests when providing their evidence. The immunity extends not merely to the oral evidence which an expert gives in court[9] but also to his reports. In *Stanton v. Callaghan*[10] Lord Justice Chadwick said:

> What then is the position in respect of experts' reports? It seems to me that the following propositions are supported by binding authority in this court:
>
> (i) an expert witness who gives evidence at trial is immune from suit in respect of anything which he says in court, and that immunity will extend to the contents of the report which he adopts as, or incorporates in, his evidence;
> (ii) where an expert witness gives evidence at trial the immunity which he would enjoy in respect of that evidence is not to be circumvented by a suit based on the report itself.

6 See Part 35 of the Civil Procedure Rules.
7 See *Stevens* v. *Gullis* [2000] 1 AER 527.
8 For a good example of this see *Royal Brompton NHS Trust* v. *Hammond (No. 7)* at 167–70.
9 See *Palmer* v. *Durnford Ford* [1992] QB 483.
10 [2000] 1 QB 75 at 100.

Importantly, certain pre-trial work which is intimately connected with his evidence also provides immunity. This kind of pre-trial work includes experts meeting, where an expert may make concessions in respect of his evidence which his client may view as seriously undermining his case. However, it is in the public interest that in such situations the expert should be free to carry out his obligations to the court. In *Stanton* Lord Justice Chadwick explained the situation as follows:

> It is important to the administration of justice, and to those members of the public who seek access to justice, that trials should take no longer than is necessary to do justice in the particular case, and that, to that end, time in court should not be taken up with the consideration of matters which are not truly at issue. It is in that context that experts are encouraged to identify, in advance of the trial, those parts of their evidence on which they are, and those on which they are not, in agreement. Provision for a joint statement, reflecting agreement after a meeting of experts has taken place, is made by RSC Order 38, r. 38. In my view the public interest in facilitating full and frank discussion between experts before trial does require that each should be free to make proper concessions without fear that any departure from advice previously given to the party who has retained him will be seen as evidence of negligence. That, as it seems to me, is an area in which public policy justifies immunity. The immunity is needed in order to avoid the tension between a desire to assist the court and fear of the consequences of a departure from previous advice.

However, that is not to say that the client who retains an expert witness cannot sue the expert in any circumstances. It is very common for a client to retain an expert in order to obtain a preliminary view prior to asking the expert to provide a formal report. On the basis of that preliminary advice the client may well decide whether to contest the case or whether to seek to compromise it. Such preliminary advices are not covered by experts' immunity, being prepared for the benefit of the client alone. The expert is required to prepare such advices with reasonable care and skill, and if he fails to comply with this obligation and the client suffers loss as a result he may be sued. Of course the practical problem facing clients in this situation is that it is usually very difficult to say that an expert providing an opinion on the facts of any particular case acted negligently even though at the end of the day his opinion may turn out to have been wrong.

Causation, loss and damage

Claims consultants and expert witnesses raise similar considerations in respect of the loss and damage which may be caused by their breaches of duty and the types of compensation which may be recovered from them by the client. In essence, because their functions are concerned with advancing the client's legal case, the loss and damage which flow from breaches of duty usually concern an alleged weakening of that case or the expense of unsuccessful litigation. Proving such losses is generally not straightforward. For example, suppose that a claims consultant carelessly gathers evidence in support of a contractor's claim for an extension of time and loss and expense, omitting to obtain vital information, and when the claim is presented at an arbitration it fails. The employer may want to claim damages for the loss of a chance that the claim would have succeeded and for the loss of the chance that he would not have had to pay the employer's legal costs and would have had his own costs paid. However, in order to do so he would have to prove not only that the claims consultant could have obtained the information, but that the information would have made a real difference to the outcome of the case and that he would have had a real chance of winning. Similarly if an expert witness negligently advises a professional that he has a good chance of successfully defending the claim made against him and the claim succeeds equally, the professional may wish to claim that given the right advice he would have settled the claim for less than the eventual judgment and would have had to pay less costs. However, he will have to prove not merely that, given the right advice, he would have attempted to settle the case but that there was a substantial chance that the claimant would have settled for less and that costs would have been saved. These kinds of causation difficulties, together with experts' immunity, often mean that although clients may feel let down by claims consultants and expert witnesses they very rarely take legal proceedings against them.

Practical considerations in actions against claims consultants and expert witnesses

1 *Form of contract.* A claims consultant will often be a quantity surveyor by training. Occasionally he will be an engineer or an architect. Sometimes, albeit rarely, he may have no professional qualification at all. However, even if qualified in one of these disciplines his services will not be engaged on the basis of a standard contract as provided by any of the professional bodies. Rather he is likely to be engaged according to a bespoke contract to provide claims consultancy services. Such a contract will contain an express or implied obligation to exercise reasonable skill and care, but it is unlikely to contain any of the other terms familiar in construction contracts as to the resolution of disputes. Similarly an expert witness although he be an architect, quantity surveyor or engineer will be engaged not on a standard contract but by means of letter of instruction from the client's solicitor. Such letters will not expressly require the exercise of reasonable skill and care and the obligation will always be implicit.

2 *Proving breach of duty.* In almost every instance it will be necessary for the person who proposes taking action against either a claims consultant

or an expert witness to obtain an expert opinion from someone qualified and practising either as a claims consultant or in the discipline in which the expert witness sought to give his evidence. In respect of claims consultants this can raise special difficulties, as the profession is new and thinly spread. This opinion will generally be required before proceedings are commenced. A professional defending such proceedings will generally also require an expert opinion. Moreover, as noted above, there are usually special difficulties in proving that a breach of duty caused loss.

3   *Insurance.* Because they are unregulated by any professional body there is no obligation upon claims consultants to carry professional indemnity insurance (although the reputable ones generally do). Consequently it will always be a consideration in any potential proceedings against claims consultants as to whether they are adequately insured. Most expert witnesses will be covered by the terms of their professional indemnity insurance for claims made in respect of breaches of duty when acting as expert witnesses.

4   *Adjudication and arbitration.* Claims consultants and expert witnesses cannot be subject to statutory adjudication and their contracts of retainer are most unlikely to contain any sort of arbitration agreement. The proper route of recovery if alternative dispute resolution fails is litigation (see Chapter 7).

5   *Limitation periods.* As will all construction professionals, claims consultants and expert witnesses owe their employers a tortious duty of care which is usually the mirror image of the contractual duty of care. Employers may seek to rely upon the tortious duty in situations where, because more than six years has elapsed between the breach of duty and the commencement of proceedings, the claim in contract would be barred by the operation of Section 5 of the Limitation Act 1980 but the employer can none the less show that damage was first suffered within time or can rely upon Section 14A of that Act (see Chapter 1).

7   Dispute resolution

The nature of dispute resolution involving allegations against construction professionals has been transformed since 1999 when a new style of litigation was introduced. The Civil Procedure Rules, which came into force in April 1999, were intended to remove the unnecessarily adversarial aspects of litigation and to require the parties to a dispute to attempt to ensure that litigation was the last resort after all cheaper and quicker avenues of dispute resolution had been considered. Potential parties to a dispute were required to discuss the nature and scope of the dispute in candid correspondence with a view to narrowing differences and seeking common ground. Alternative dispute resolution techniques such as mediation and conciliation were to be encouraged. Litigation itself was to be both less technical and more open, with the courts keeping a keen eye on the parties to ensure that they did not take too long or incur unacceptable costs. The new mood has had an impact on the way in which all disputes involving construction professionals are conducted, increasing the early exchange of important information between parties, increasing the availability of informal structures aimed at promoting settlement, limiting some of the uncertainties in litigation and substantially reducing not merely the time and costs of litigation but also the number of cases going to trial.

Pre-action steps and alternative dispute resolution

Before any dispute involving construction professionals reaches the stage of legal proceedings there is usually a lengthy genesis during which the likely claim is identified, evidence is assembled, the merits of the claim are considered and the nature of the claim is formulated. This process may involve claims consultants or solicitors from the very beginning or they may become involved only at the latter stages. There may be extensive correspondence on the subject matter of the proposed claim with the professional, or alternatively the first the professional may learn of the proposed claim is when he receives a formal letter of claim (see below). Sometimes claims are intimated against professionals only after the professional has unsuccessfully sought payment of his fees and has threatened litigation.

Pre-action steps

It is helpful to consider this 'pre-claim' period from the perspective of a potential claimant and from the perspective of a professional. The claimant will usually be an employer who is aggrieved about some aspect of the professional's work. For example the construction contract may have sustained substantial time overruns or large additional costs by way of variation instructions and the employer may be dissatisfied with the explanation which is provided for these by his architect; some feature of the design may have failed – a load-bearing wall may have been found to be inadequate, the steelwork may not have been compatible with the curtain walling; substantial instances of defective work may emerge long after the architect has certified compliance with the defects liability period requirements. In response to these problems the employer is likely to contact a solicitor. By this stage he may or may not have dispensed with the services of the professional and engaged a replacement. He will usually be advised to obtain a preliminary expert's report identifying the nature and cause of the problem and, importantly, the steps required to rectify it together with some estimate of the costs of those steps. In order to enable the solicitor to instruct the expert and further to advise the employer the latter will usually be asked to provide the solicitor with such relevant documents and records as he possesses. The solicitor may also ask for statements from key personnel as to important factual matters – what they were told, what they agreed to, when damage first became apparent and so forth. In cases where the problem comes to light long after the works have finished the employer may not have retained much of this documentation and the recollections of his key personnel can be patchy. In the usual case the solicitor will advise his client that a claim should be intimated against a professional only after all this information has been considered together with the views of any expert who has been asked to report. Consequently it is not untypical for a claim to be intimated months or even years after a problem has come to light.

The construction professional may be unaware that a claim is being prepared against him until he receives a letter from the claimant's solicitor. However, in many cases the problem will have become clear whilst the work was progressing and the professional will become aware from an early stage of the possibility that action may be taken against him. As discussed in Chapter 2, most policies of professional indemnity insurance require professionals to notify their insurers at a very early stage when they become aware that a claim may be made against them. Certainly it is prudent to provide such early notification even if the professional takes the view that the problem may be resolved or may never result in a formal claim. The insurer will usually require to be kept informed of developments and may caution the professional about making any admissions in meetings or in correspondence which might weaken the insurer's ability to defend any claim. Even if no claim has been intimated, the professional should take special care to ensure that his records are as complete as they can be and that all notes, correspondence, memoranda, e-mails, site diaries and other information which might be relevant to any future dispute are retained.

In the usual situation of a claim being made against a construction professional, the claimant will set out his claim in detail in a 'pre-action letter.' This is the first step in the sequence prescribed in the 'Pre-action Protocol for Construction and Engineering Disputes' which governs, amongst other claims, claims against construction professionals.[1] The aim of the protocol is to ensure that the parties to potential legal proceedings fully ventilate their grievances in correspondence with a view to maximising the prospects of resolving the dispute before it reaches the courts and if the claim does reach the courts to support efficient case management. The recommended steps are as follows: After receipt of the detailed letter of claim the professional is required to produce a detailed response, including any counterclaim (for example for unpaid fees). The potential claimant then provides his detailed response to that letter. Where appropriate relevant documents should be provided accompanying these letters. After the exchange of correspondence between the parties there should be one or more 'without prejudice' meetings so that the parties can seek to identify the issues in their dispute, identify the root cause of disagreement in respect of each issue and consider how the dispute might be resolved without the need for recourse to litigation or, if litigation cannot be avoided, decide how best it should be conducted so as to minimise delay and expense and otherwise assist in the promotion of efficient litigation. Failure to follow the Protocol may result in a party to litigation being ordered to pay costs arising out of its unreasonable behaviour.[2]

Alternative dispute resolution

The essential distinction between alternative dispute resolution (ADR) and adjudication, arbitration or litigation (see below) is that, for the most part, ADR is a voluntary process in which the parties engage because they both want to arrive at a settlement. The parties submit themselves to a structured process which lacks the formality and the safeguards of litigation or arbitration but which is intended to narrow the differences between them and provide assistance to their efforts to compromise. Its advantages are that it is invariably quicker and cheaper than litigation. The vast majority of professional negligence cases involving construction professionals settle before they reach court, often after substantial costs have been incurred. ADR offers a route by which most of those costs can be saved. Its disadvantage is that in order to be successful it requires a genuine desire on the part of the

---

1 This is a protocol under the Civil Procedure Rules which came into force on 2 October 2000.
2 See for example *Paul Thomas Construction Ltd* v. *Hyland* 2002 Con LJ 345.

participants to reach an agreement. This is not always the case. A client who believes that his engineer was totally to blame for the consequences of a defective design may have no desire to engage in a process whereby he ends up agreeing to recover less than his full entitlement.

There are various forms of ADR, including judicial appraisal, expert determination, conciliation and mediation.[3] Of all these, mediation is by far the most common and the most likely to be encountered by construction professionals (although it should be noted that the RIBA operates a conciliation procedure to which specific reference is made in clause 9.1 of the Standard Form of Agreement for the Appointment of an Architect). Mediation consists of a structured meeting conducted by a trained *mediator* whose object is to encourage the parties to take note of each other's points and arrive at a settlement. Such trained mediators usually operate under the auspices of a mediation body which specialises in providing ADR services, for example the Centre for Dispute Resolution. Typically the mediation might begin by both parties preparing statements of their position. These are encouraged to be open, positive and constructive rather than protective and adversarial. The statements tell each party and the mediator what is common ground and which issues are likely to require negotiation. After a brief joint meeting, the mediator may begin the work of mediation by shuttling between the parties who are located in separate rooms, discussing with each their weak and strong points and identifying possible solutions or factors which might feature in a settlement. At a later stage the mediator might bring the parties together and encourage face-to-face dialogue, followed by another round of shuttling. In a successful mediation the parties reach an agreement which is then recorded so that it can be formally expressed in legal documents to be drafted later. Even an unsuccessful mediation can result in a narrowing of the dispute between the parties and may make considerable progress towards an eventual settlement. The entire mediation process is conducted 'without prejudice': that is, neither party is entitled to reveal to a court or arbitrator what was said or done in the course of the mediation until the case has been decided and the only remaining issues concern the costs of the proceedings. This is to encourage the parties to be candid in their conduct of the mediation and particularly to make concessions or admissions which they would be otherwise reluctant to make for fear of harming their prospects in litigation or arbitration.

Mediation (or other form of ADR) can involve any number of parties and can take place at any stage in the general dispute resolution process. Ideally it should be pursued prior to the commencement of litigation. However, it is very common for litigation to be commenced and statements of case exchanged (see below) and for the parties then to agree that the case

---

3 The Technology and Construction Solicitors' Association provides a useful ADR protocol which can be found on its web site at www.tecsaorg.uk.

be 'stayed' – that is, an order issued that no further steps be taken – whilst the parties mediate in an attempt to resolve some or all of the issues between them. The courts encourage mediation and it has become increasing common for judges to apply pressure to the parties to go to mediation and to punish parties in costs if they have acted unreasonably in refusing to engage in this or any other ADR process. One study[4] suggests a settlement rate of about 65 per cent of all professional negligence cases involving construction professionals going to mediation and it is to be anticipated that this 'success' rate may rise as those involved in the construction industry, their insurers and their lawyers become more familiar with and more adept in using the mediation process.

The commencement of legal proceedings

The term 'legal proceedings' is used here to denote a compulsory adversarial legal dispute, conducted before an independent tribunal such as an adjudicator, arbitrator or judge who has the power to decide in favour of one party to the proceedings and make awards which will lead to compensation being paid. The three forms of such legal proceedings which involve construction professionals are adjudication, arbitration and litigation. In the vast majority of professional negligence disputes the professional can be expected to rely upon his lawyer, usually funded by his insurers, to act on his behalf and guide him through the complexities of legal proceedings. Nevertheless it is important for the professional involved in legal proceedings to be aware of what they consist of and how they may involve him. With the exception of adjudication (see below) most of professional negligence cases involving construction professionals reach the stage of legal proceedings only after the expiry of the pre-action period discussed above. Consequently – and ideally – a professional negligence claim against a construction professional should reach the stage of being arbitrated or litigated only when the parties have failed to reach an accommodation, notwithstanding that they are both aware of at least an outline of the substantial strengths and weaknesses of each other's case.

However, not every claim against professionals will follow this route. Occasionally claims against professionals are discovered close to the expiry of the limitation period (see Chapter 1) or at a time where it is unclear whether the limitation period has expired or not. In these circumstances the party wishing to make the claim will often commence proceedings immediately so as to protect his position. In the usual course the parties will then agree a stay of proceedings so that the steps advocated by the Pre-action Protocol can be followed. If this happens the parties will have time to explore the strengths and weaknesses of each other's case and possibly attempt to

---

4 'Construction lawyers' attitudes and experiences with ADR', 2002 Con LJ 97.

reach a compromise before any further steps in the litigation are taken. Sometimes a professional will be aware that his client is unhappy about some aspect of his performance but will not be expressly informed as to the precise cause of the difficulty until he seeks payment of his fees. Indeed sometimes the client will not make any assertion of professional negligence until the professional has commenced proceedings to recover his fees. This situation may arise because the client has not at that stage been able to identify whether the professional or some other party is responsible for his difficulty or alternatively is not sure whether the alleged breach of duty will cause substantial loss (for example in respect of alleged negligent certification where the employer may yet recover monies overpaid from the contractor). In these instances the employer's hand is forced by action for fees and the result may be that the claim against the professional is not as well thought out and prepared as it should be. Moreover this may be the first opportunity which the professional has had to notify his insurers. He will need time to consider the situation, instruct panel solicitors and investigate the allegations. Consequently it is common that in this situation the parties will seek to agree a stay whilst the matters raised by the professional negligence allegations can be investigated. Lastly, the claim against the professional may be brought by some person who is being sued and who wishes to seek contribution from the professional or some other remedy in relation to the matters being litigated against him. Such proceedings are known as Part 20 proceedings (see Chapter 1). For example, an employer may sue his structural engineer concerning alleged defects in design advice. The structural engineer may then commence Part 20 proceedings against the architect, alleging that his negligent advice to the client was also to blame. Alternatively a contractor may claim against an employer that he has not received his proper entitlement under the building contract in respect of additional work caused by design variations. The employer may wish to defend these proceedings but none the less to sue the architect for negligently preparing an original design which was defective and which had to be varied mid-way through the course of the work in order to correct the defects. If brought into legal proceedings in this way the professional may find himself required to take legal steps such as preparing and serving a defence (see below) without the benefit of the pre-action preparation. Indeed the action may move relatively speedily to trial, leaving the professional and his advisers having to work hard to 'catch up'.

Adjudication

The process of adjudication is arguably an exception to the recent trend favouring the promotion of compromise in that it provides a mechanism whereby one party to a building contract can seek a decision from an adjudicator that the other party, amongst other things, should pay compensation. This decision can be obtained within a matter of weeks on the basis of a perfunctory procedure, is enforceable almost immediately and remains in place until a court or arbitrator comes to a different view. The system of statutory adjudication was introduced by the Housing Grants Construction and Regeneration Act 1996 (HGCRA). It was intended to provide a very quick and cheap, if rough-and-ready, method of determining the entitlements of parties to a construction dispute and was in part intended to allow the parties to a building contract to reach a rapid, if temporary, resolution of a dispute. Whilst principally directed at traditional disputes between employers and contractors it can and does have application to disputes with construction professionals. Although uncommon it is employed by both claimants against professionals and professionals themselves when judged to be tactically in their interests.

Unless the contract already contains a satisfactory adjudication procedure (which, architects and engineers apart,[5] is unlikely in respect of contracts with construction professionals) the HGCRA implies a term that the adjudication provisions of the Scheme for Construction Contracts apply. Either party can refer the dispute to adjudication by service of a notice which prompts the appointment of an adjudicator. The adjudicator may be a lawyer but is more likely to be an architect, engineer, surveyor or other construction professional. Within the notice of adjudication the referring party sets out its full case, together with supporting documents, in a referral notice. The adjudicator will then give directions to the parties as to the future conduct of the adjudication. Usually these will consist of requiring a response from the defending party within a very tight time frame (generally no more than two weeks). The adjudicator will then consider the evidence and the parties' submissions. Often this will be an exercise entirely carried out on the basis of the documents submitted to him, although sometimes he will agree to hear oral submissions. The adjudicator must reach a decision no later than twenty-eight days after receiving the referral notice unless the timetable has been extended by agreement. Occasionally the adjudicator will ask for an oral hearing, but the more common procedure is for him to decide the dispute on the basis of the documents alone. The decision of the adjudicator is binding upon the parties and may be enforced by summary procedure in court (typically an order that a sum of money must be paid by one party to the other). Unless specifically provided for in the contract, he has no power to award costs or interest.[6] The decision of an adjudicator is extremely difficult to challenge by way of appeal and otherwise remains binding until the same

---

5 See for example clause 9.2 of the RIBA Standard Form of Agreement for the Appointment of an Architect (SFA/99) and clause 9.2 of the ACE Conditions of Engagement – Agreement A(1).

6 Clause 9.2 of the RIBA Standard Form of Agreement for the Appointment of an Architect (SFA/99) provides for the use of the adjudication scheme as set out in the Model Adjudication Procedures published by the Construction Industry Council, modified so as to permit the adjudicator to make an award of costs. However, in respect of other professionals whether the adjudicator has the power to award costs will depend upon whether the parties have agreed that he should.

issues are litigated or arbitrated and judgment is given or an award made. His decision can be enforced in summary proceedings in court.

The chief reasons for seeking to adjudicate a dispute between a construction professional and his employer are tactical. The construction professional may take the view that the employer's purported complaints of professional negligence are groundless and that an adjudicator is likely to award the professional his fees and dismiss those complaints. An employer may take the view that his negotiating position with a professional's insurers will be strengthened if he succeeds at adjudication and that the element of surprise and the short response time available to the professional greatly increases his prospects of success. Adjudication is unusual in that it represents the only area where parties are not discouraged from resolving their differences by adversarial proceedings before they have taken the opportunity to see if they can reach agreement. The process does not always result in saving costs or time and has many critics. Its usefulness in the context of professional negligence disputes is doubtful and it is generally unsuitable for complex disputes or disputes where the sums of money in issue are substantial. As a rule of thumb there will be few instances where either the employer or the professional will find it a beneficial remedy.

Arbitration

Arbitration is a form of adversarial dispute resolution where the parties agree to submit to the jurisdiction of an individual selected by them (or in default of agreement nominated by a third party) who will conduct the proceedings between them and issue a decision which will bind them. In contrast to ADR it is a form of semi-compulsory private litigation because the parties are required to arbitrate if they have signed an arbitration clause and at least one of them decides that the dispute should be arbitrated. It takes proceedings which would otherwise have been conducted publicly through the courts and places them under private auspices. Sir John Donaldson MR characterised the process in this way:

> Arbitration is usually no more and no less than litigation in the private sector. The arbitrator is called upon to find the facts, apply the law and grant relief to one or other or both of the parties.[7]

Some construction professionals' standard Forms of Engagement contain voluntary arbitration clauses. Quantity surveyors engaged pursuant to the RICS terms and conditions attached to the Form of Inquiry and Fee Quotation are subject to a voluntary arbitration provision under clause 12.1, which states:

---

7 *Northern RHA* v. *Derek Crouch* [1984] QB 644 at 670.

Any dispute arising under this Agreement, including those for more than £50,000 and/or those where adjudication would not apply, may be referred at the instance of either of the parties to be determined by an arbitrator.

By contrast, clause 9.5 of the RIBA Standard Form of Agreement for the Appointment of an Architect (SFA/99) states:

When in accordance with Article 5 either the Client or the Architect require any dispute or difference to be referred to arbitration the requiring party shall give notice to the other to such effect and the dispute or difference shall be referred to the arbitration and final decision of a person to be agreed between the parties. . . .

Article 5 allows the parties to select compulsory arbitration rather than litigation as the adversarial means of resolving disputes (apart from adjudication). If the selection is made, either the architect or the employer may force the other to arbitrate rather than go to court. The various ACE Conditions of Engagement for Engineers also contain arbitration provisions. Of course it is open to either party to a proposed agreement containing a compulsory arbitration clause to delete this clause prior to contract and, as with all arbitration agreements, if neither party seeks arbitration or one party waives its rights to insist on arbitration there can be no compulsion to take this route. It is increasingly common for architects and/or their clients not to make use of Article 5 or any equivalent arbitration clause when entering into appointments, and some quantity surveyors and engineers and their clients similarly decline to employ the standard arbitration provision in their agreements. Moreover construction professionals who are joined as Part 20 defendants to multi-party litigation sometimes cannot or choose not to insist on their right to have the dispute referred to arbitration. Consequently, notwithstanding the presence of standard arbitration clauses, it may be that actions against construction professionals are as frequently litigated as arbitrated.

An arbitration is commenced by a notice describing the nature of the dispute. The notice prompts the appointment of an arbitrator, who is normally chosen by the parties. Typically they will provide each other with a list of names and seek to agree a candidate. The background of the arbitrator is also a matter of choice – he may be a lawyer or an architect or an engineer or a surveyor, depending upon the nature of the dispute and the parties' own perception of their best interests. In professional negligence disputes it would be usual to appoint a professional in the relevant discipline. In default of agreement arbitration clauses usually provide for an arbitrator to be selected by the relevant professional body – in the case of architects the RIBA. The arbitrator is appointed by the parties who are responsible for his costs. However, he is required to act impartially and will generally take pains to be seen to be acting even-handedly – for example by insisting that any correspondence between himself and one party is copied to the other party. The arbitrator will usually hold a meeting so as to give directions to the parties. These may mimic the directions which would be given in proceedings conducted in court and will include the exchange of statements of case, the disclosure of documentation, the exchange of witness statements, the exchange of experts reports' and so on (see below). However, one of the virtues of arbitration is that the arbitrator is not bound by such procedures and is encouraged to find ways of minimising delay and expense.[8] Consequently it is common for arbitrators to direct a course which suits the parties and which is designed to get quickly to the heart of the matters in issue.

In a complex arbitration it is common to have a number of hearings in front of an arbitrator and for him to break up his decisions into a series of interim awards. However, for most cases involving professionals it would be usual for there to be one hearing at which oral evidence was taken from both witnesses and experts with a view to enabling the arbitrator to reach a final award. The arbitrator can make any award that might be open to a Court. In the context of professional negligence actions this usually means the payment of monies – either fees payable from the employer to the professional or damages payable by the professional to the employer. However, it should be noted that the arbitrator has the power to award interest and to decide costs – being both the question of which party pays his fees and which party will pay the other party's costs. There are rules allowing the parties to make offers similar to Part 36 payments and offers in litigation (see below). Appeal from an arbitrator's decision is very difficult: the court will agree to hear an appeal only if the arbitrator's decision was 'obviously wrong' or raises some question of public importance and the decision is at least open to serious doubt.[9] Whilst the conduct of arbitrations is regulated by statute[10] the policy of the courts is to intervene as little as possible, the parties having agreed to take the dispute out of the judicial arena and litigate it privately. For this reason, outside of clear cases of bias or gross errors of procedure or law, the courts will not generally interfere with the conduct of an arbitration by an arbitrator.

Arbitration can be preferable to court proceedings in that it is private and more flexible. The first of these considerations may be important to both employers and professionals, who would not wish commercially sensitive information to be deployed in open court or who wish to avoid adverse publicity. Arbitration is also more flexible because as a rule the arbitrator acts at the behest of the parties and can tailor his directions to suit them. If

---

8 See Section 33 of the Arbitration Act 1996.
9 Section 69 (3) Arbitration Act 1996.
10 Arbitration Act 1996.

they wish to put the arbitration 'on hold' for commercial reasons which they do not wish to disclose to the arbitrator there is generally no difficulty (subject to his other commitments). In contrast the procedure of the courts is dictated by the interests of justice rather than the parties' convenience and parties frequently find that judges direct that cases are brought to trial on dates earlier than suit either of them. Lastly there is often thought to be an advantage in very technical cases in having an architect, engineer or surveyor as an arbitrator. However, arbitration can suffer from substantial disadvantages as against court proceedings. The chief disadvantage is that, because arbitrations are founded on contractual rights, there is no power in an arbitrator to seek to involve third parties in the arbitration proceedings. Many disputes between employers and construction professionals involve third parties. Either the employer or the professional may want to involve the contractor or other professionals as Part 20 defendants or, in a dispute between an employer and a contractor, either party may wish to join the professional as a Part 20 defendant. Unless all parties and the arbitrator agree this is impossible in arbitration proceedings. Secondly professional negligence proceedings often involve difficult issues of law. Such issues are often better suited to the courts than to arbitration (even where the arbitrator is legal qualified) because the scope of the right to appeal is so much broader in the courts. It is probably these disadvantages which lead professionals such as architects frequently decline to include compulsory arbitration clauses in their contracts.

Litigation

Litigation is the most common form of legal proceedings in which professional negligence actions against construction professionals are resolved. These proceedings are conducted in open court (i.e. in public) in front of a judge. The location and type of court will depend upon the nature of the claim against the professional and how it arose. If the court action merely involves the professional and his employer the determining factors will be the value of the claim and the claimant's choice of venue. Many claims against professionals arise by reason of the professional being a second defendant. In actions where the estimated claim is relatively small (that is, usually worth less than £30,000),[11] proceedings are often brought in the County Court nearest to the claimant's address. However, most professional negligence claims against construction professionals are thought to be unsuitable for County Court proceedings because of their specialised subject matter and unless the claim has a very low value it is more commonly litigated in one of

---

11 This is because the higher costs of High Court proceedings may not be thought to be justified by claims with a value below this figure, which is the multi-track minimum. Actions where the value of the claim is less than £15,000 *must* be taken in the County Court.

the Technology and Construction Courts (TCC), the largest being in London, but others being present in the major cities.[12] The TCC is a specialist part of the High Court which provides judges experienced in technical matters and in particular judges possessing expertise in construction litigation. Where, as is often the case, the claim is being taken as part of proceedings involving more than one party – for example where the professional is one of a number of defendants – it would be unusual for legal proceedings to take place in any other court.

The claim

The litigation process is commenced by the issue of a *claim form*. This is a short formal document which contains a very brief summary of the claimant's complaint and the remedy he is seeking. The special significance of issuing a claim form is that the date of issue is not merely the commencement of litigation but also the date from which limitation is judged (see Chapter 1). The claim form may be served up to four months after issue. Depending on the status of the professional at the date when the alleged breach of duty occurred and the way in which the claimant chooses to sue him a professional who is or was a member of a partnership can be sued in his own name or in the name of the partnership. In the usual case the claim form will be served upon the defendant professional's solicitors, who will have agreed to accept service on his behalf.

The statements of case

Once the claim form has been served, the defendant professional (through his solicitor) will formally acknowledge service. This is the trigger for the claimant to serve its *particulars of claim*, which is the document in which it sets out the precise nature of its complaint and the precise remedy it seeks. The particulars of claim may well have been prepared by a barrister instructed by the claimant's solicitors. At this point the defendant professional's solicitors will set about the preparation of a *defence*, which is the document in which the defendant professional will seek to meet, point by point, the issues raised by the claimant and to raise any other points which it wishes the court to consider. During this period the defendant professional can expect to be consulted as to the proposed contents of the defence. If he has not already done so, he may be asked to prepare a statement setting out his recollection of certain events. There is often a substantial delay in the provision of a defence in order to allow the defendant professional's solicitors time to instruct an expert to advise them as to technical matters raised (see below), although in many cases, particularly those involving substantial sums, an

---

12 Manchester, Leeds, Newcastle, Bristol and Cardiff.

expert will already have been retained. The defendant professional's solicitors will often send the papers to a barrister so that he can draft the defence and advise. Occasionally the defendant professional will be asked to attend a meeting with the barrister (a 'conference') so that he can ask questions of the professional and give him advice face-to-face. Prior to the defence being served the defendant professional (or, if his firm or company is being sued, a partner director or some other suitable person) will be asked to sign a *statement of truth* attached to the defence verifying the truth of its contents. From time to time the parties to the litigation may be required to amplify or clarify their case by the provision of further particulars. All these documents taken together provide the framework which guides the parties and the court as to which are the issues to be tried and what each party says in relation to them. They are referred to as the *statements of case*. A party will usually not be allowed to advance a contention at trial if it has not been previously raised in his statement of case.

Case management

One of the distinguishing features of the TCC is that the judges have always taken a very 'hands-on' role in 'case management', that is, they take trouble to ensure that the parties come to court at an early stage in the proceedings so that the issues of where the case is going and how it can be most economically and efficiently progressed are considered. Each case is allocated to an individual judge who will 'manage' that case in all its stages up to trial and then will hear the trial itself. There may be a number of such hearings throughout the course of the litigation which may variously be referred to as 'directions hearings', 'case management conferences' and 'pre-trial reviews'. Thus after the service of the defence the judge will usually require the parties' lawyers to attend so that he can give directions as to the future conduct of the case. It is not usual for the professional concerned to attend these directions hearings, although sometimes it happens. At this stage it sometimes happens that one party will seek a special hearing to determine a particular issue in the litigation by the summary method[13] where he may succeed on that issue provided he can show that the other party has no real prospect of succeeding upon the issue and there is no other substantial reason why it should go to full trial. More generally the parties and the court will give consideration as to whether in the interests of saving time and costs there are any specific issues which can safely be heard in advance of the others. Sometimes if one party relies upon a limitation argument that issue is ordered to be heard as a preliminary issue. Where the issues of breach of duty and causation and quantum can be safely split from each other the court may order that the allegation of breach of duty is heard as a preliminary issue. In

13 CPR Part 24.

actions concerning a number of defendants, not all of whom are involved in the same allegations, the court may look for ways of structuring the action so as to hear certain parts of the case in advance of others. When providing these directions the court will have regard to balancing the need to have the case tried promptly against the time reasonably required by all the parties to prepare themselves so as to be in a position adequately to contest the proceedings. Construction litigation has traditionally been very time-consuming and expensive, and professional negligence actions involving construction professionals are no exception. However, particularly since the advent of the CPR the courts have been unwilling to tolerate delay on the part of parties to such litigation and whilst it is not uncommon for litigation involving construction professionals to take two years or longer to come to trial the period between the commencement of proceedings and the handing down of judgment has become shorter and shorter.

A further feature of current litigation in the TCC is the encouragement given by the judges to ADR. Even though the parties may have unsuccessfully attempted to resolve their differences previously judges in the TCC will usually want to know whether fresh consideration has been given to the prospects of resolving the case by mediation or some other suitable method. If there is a reasonable prospect of a successful outcome by this means the Court will usually grant a stay of proceedings – for example for three months – to allow the parties time to attempt to compromise. Indeed some judges offer to provide ADR services, which can be particularly useful where the parties are divided on difficult issues of law.

Disclosure

One of the most important steps likely to be directed by the court is disclosure. English litigation is characterised by a 'cards on the table' approach where each side is required to disclose to the other such documents as it has in its possession which may advance or damage its case or advance or damage the case of any other party to the proceedings. Thus, for example, the internal memoranda held by an employer may have a crucial bearing on allegations that the employer did or did not give certain instructions or was or was not aware of certain concerns expressed by the professional. By the same token the engineer may possess drawings or sketches which have an important bearing upon whether he was aware of certain features of the site or whether he made certain errors in his calculations. Sometimes the most important documents are notes of conversations where the parties are in dispute as to what was said. Because these are usually contemporaneous and written at a time long before any dispute had become apparent the courts tend to regard them as a good guide as to what really happened. However, very often the importance of documents lies in the overall impression they provide – for example a generally sloppy approach by a professional or a cavalier approach to risk by an employer – and to what is not there so much as what is – for example the absence of a currently advanced explanation or justification from earlier correspondence in which it might be expected to appear. Even in professional negligence actions, which as a rule are less reliant upon documentary records than other types of construction litigation, the importance of contemporaneous documentation cannot be overestimated. For this reason parties to litigation come under an immediate duty to preserve all such documentation as may become the subject of disclosure pending a direction for that disclosure.[14] In providing disclosure – the process whereby his solicitor makes lists of all disclosable documents and permits the other party's solicitor to inspect and take copies of them – the professional may be required to affirm that he has carried out a proper search for all such documents and otherwise complied with his obligations. As a general rule, the only documents which although highly material need not be disclosed are those where the professional is writing to or being written to by his solicitor for the purpose of obtaining legal advice and some documents which are generated in the litigation process itself.

Witness statements

The next stage in the litigation is for the parties to exchange *witness statements* of the witnesses of fact. In keeping with an open approach to litigation it has long been a requirement that each party discloses well in advance of any trial what its witnesses will say in evidence. Indeed because their statements are intended to be a complete summary of the evidence they intend to give advocates acting for the party calling the witness will not generally be permitted to ask supplementary questions to elicit evidence which could and should have been contained in a witness statement. Consequently the professional can expect to be asked by his solicitor to comment on a draft witness statement which has been prepared on his behalf based upon his previous statement or statements, letters, reports and information provided in meetings. Frequently the statement will be lengthy and it may refer to many documents. Great care should always be taken by the professional in approving such a statement as it will constitute his evidence to the court and he will be required to affirm the truth of its contents. Witness statements are normally exchanged simultaneously so that neither party has the advantage or seeing the contents of the other side's statements before he prepares his own. Once exchange has taken place the professional will usually be provided with copies of the other parties' witness statements so that he can understand what is being said by them and can provide helpful information to his lawyers.

14 A defendant professional's solicitor will usually have requested the contents of the professional's files at an earlier stage in order to consider them. However, he may have returned them to the professional, having taken copies of material documents. He will usually give advice as to the professional's obligation to preserve all relevant documentation.

Experts' reports

The exchange of witness statements is usually followed by the exchange of experts' reports. As discussed in Chapter 1 the role of experts can be crucial in professional negligence actions against construction professionals. They not only guide the court as to the technical considerations to be kept in mind when considering whether there has been a breach of duty, but also provide evidence of the standard of care to be expected in the relevant profession and (depending on the discipline) they may also provide opinion relevant to causation and quantum. Although experts are retained by the parties they are expected to provide an objective opinion to the court – they should not enter into the arena in order to advocate their client's case.[15] For this reason whilst it is quite proper for him to consult his client and his lawyers he should not allow either of them to put words in his mouth. Quite often the professional may be unhappy that his expert appears to be taking a less robust line than he believes is justified. However, whilst it is permissible for the client and the lawyer to question the expert and raise particular issues and arguments with him, it is quite impermissible to attempt to persuade him to take a particular standpoint. Moreover it should be noted that whilst experts who approach their work with scrupulous care and independence tend to impress judges, experts who have allowed themselves to be swayed by their clients into taking a partisan view tend to create an adverse reaction often highly damaging to their client's prospects of success. The process of preparing expert evidence begins with the exchange of experts' reports. The court will probably direct the experts to meet after that exchange to see what areas of their reports can be agreed and to otherwise narrow the areas of disagreement. They may be asked to carry out further tests or inspections. After the completion of this process they may be required to prepare further reports dealing with the areas of disagreement and setting out their responses to each other's initial reports.

Trial

Once the expert evidence is complete a case will usually be ready for trial. In practice the directions timetable will have allowed a short period of perhaps a few months between the conclusion of that evidence and the start of the trial. The trial itself is conducted by the claimant calling his evidence of fact, his witnesses being cross-examined, followed by the witnesses of fact of the other parties being called and cross-examined. The parties' experts will usually give their evidence last. At the conclusion of all the evidence the defence advocates will provide the court with their submissions, followed by the claimant's advocate. Except in straightforward cases the judge will

---

15 Garland J in *University of Warwick* v. *Sir Robert McAlpine* (1988) 42 BLR 1 at 22.

'reserve' his judgment, that is, he will take time to think about what he is going to decide and he will often write out a judgment which will be provided to the parties weeks or often months after the final submissions.

Costs

Once the result is known the parties will return to court to argue about any remaining matters, one of which will usually be costs. All construction litigation, including litigation against construction professionals, is very expensive. It is relatively common to come across cases where the eventual total legal costs (including the cost of the experts) exceed the damages that one party may recover. In English litigation the general rule is that the loser pays the winner's reasonable legal costs as well as bearing his own. However, in order to facilitate early settlement and promote efficient litigation a number of important rules have been introduced which deviate from that principle. The most important rules concern 'payments into court'. At any stage in proceedings being taken against him a construction professional may make a payment into court in an attempt to settle the claim. This literally involves sending a cheque to the court, which retains the money with interest accruing pending acceptance or the outcome of the case. If the payment is accepted, the claimant takes that sum and his reasonable legal costs to date in satisfaction of his claim. If the payment is not accepted[16] and the claimant receives less by way of damages and interest than represented the value of the payment in at the last date for acceptance, he will pay the defendant's costs of the action from that date.

Thus suppose that an employer claims £100,000 from a surveyor in respect of loss caused by negligent surveying. The surveyor pays £80,000 into court, the last date for acceptance being 1 March. In October the case comes to trial. If the employer is awarded £90,000 he recovers that sum and all his reasonable costs. If the employer is awarded £70,000 he recovers that sum and his costs to 1 March. However, he must pay the surveyor's reasonable costs after 1 March and bear his own costs from that date also. The fact of the payment in is kept secret from the Judge and revealed only when the court comes to consider who should be awarded the costs of the action. In most cases where a construction professional is advised by his lawyers to be at risk of a finding of breach of duty and being made to pay an award of damages he will be advised (or, in more practical terms, his insurers will be advised) to make a payment into court, which will provide some cost protection. The amount paid in may vary according to the tactical imperative.[17] However, it will often approximate to the defendant's lawyers'

---

16 The claimant has twenty-one days in which to accept it.
17 Defendants' insurers often make a low payment in so as not to set to high a threshold for subsequent negotiations.

estimation of what the case is really worth so as to provide them with a realistic chance of doing better at trial and by the same token causing the claimant sufficient concern to make him accept. Since the advent of the CPR claimants have been able to make use of a similar stratagem. Claimants can now write on a 'without prejudice' basis to a defendant making a 'Part 36 offer'. This is a sum of money which they will accept, together with their reasonable legal costs, in order to compromise the claim. If the defendant does not accept the offer and the claimant does better than the offer at trial, the claimant may be entitled to indemnity costs – that is, a higher than usual recovery of costs – and punitive rates of interest on the sum awarded since the date when the offer should have been accepted. There are no adverse consequences to a claimant who fails to beat his own Part 36 offer. Again, because the offer is made 'without prejudice' it cannot be seen by the court until after judgment has been delivered. Lastly it should be noted that even though one party may be the winner in any particular litigation he may be deprived of his costs or ordered to pay the other side's costs if the court takes the view that he has conducted any part of the litigation unreasonably or has lost on issues where significant time and expense were incurred.

Appeal

It may be possible to appeal a decision of a judge to the Court of Appeal. However, it should be noted that the appeal has to concern an error of law: except in exceptional circumstances no appeal will be available where the loser merely believes that the judge got the facts wrong. Moreover permission to appeal is required, either from the judge or from the Court of Appeal itself, either or which has to be satisfied that the appeal has reasonable prospects of success.

Appendix 1

APIA–RIBA Standard Form of Agreement for the Appointment of an Architect: policy wording, 2002

1 Definitions and Interpretation

1.1 'Assured' shall mean:

    (a) Any person or Firm for whom indemnity has been requested in the proposal form;

    (b) Any other person who has been or during the Period of Insurance becomes a partner director or principal of the Firm;

provided that liability arises directly out of Professional Business carried out by that person in the name of the Firm.

1.2 'Firm' shall mean the Assured Firm described in the Schedule.

1.3 'Professional Business' shall mean the business described in the Schedule.

1.4 'Geographical Limits' shall mean any territory within the European Union, Isle of Man and the Channel Islands or such additional territory described in the Schedule.

1.5 'Period of Insurance' shall mean the period shown in the Schedule.

1.6 'Limit of Indemnity' shall mean the sum shown in the Schedule.

    The liability of Insurers under Section 3 shall not exceed the Limit of Indemnity in respect of each and every claim (or series of claims from the same originating cause) but where any claim circumstance or event is notified to Insurers which is the same as or arises out of or is connected with any claim circumstance or event notified at the same time or previously such claim circumstance or event shall not be separate for the purposes of assessing the Limit of Indemnity available to the Assured.

    The liability of Insurers under Section 4 shall not exceed in the aggregate the sum shown in the Schedule.

1.7 'defence costs' shall mean all costs and expenses incurred with the prior written and continuing consent of the Insurers in the investigation defence or settlement of any claim circumstance or event and the costs of representation at any inquiry or other proceedings, whether civil or criminal, which have a direct impact on any claim circumstance or event which is likely to form the subject of indemnity by Insurers.

1.8 'Excess' shall mean the first amount of each claim (or series or claims from the same originating cause) shown in the Schedule, which is to be borne by the Assured.

1.9 'document' shall mean deeds, wills, agreements, maps, plans, records, written or printed books, letters, certificates or written or printed documents or forms of any nature whatsoever (excluding any bearer bonds or coupons, bank or currency notes or other negotiable paper) and/or magnetic tape or other like means of recording information for use with any computer record system.

1.10 'claim' shall mean any claim made against the Assured.

1.11 'claimant' shall mean the party making such claim.

1.12 'circumstance or event' shall mean any circumstance or event which is likely to give rise to a claim.

1.13 'United Kingdom' shall mean England, Wales, Scotland, Northern Ireland, Isle of Man and the Channel Islands.

1.14 'Internet' shall mean the worldwide group of inter-connected networks accessible via service providers or online service providers using dial-up telephone service, digital subscriber lines, integrated service digital network lines, cable modem access or similar transfer mediums.

1.15 'Intranet' shall mean one or more inter-connected networks with restricted access to the Assured via service providers or online service providers using dial-up telephone service, digital subscriber lines, integrated service digital network lines, cable modem access or similar transfer mediums.

1.16 'Extranet' shall mean a restricted-access group of inter-connected networks accessible via service providers on online service providers using dial-up telephone service, digital subscriber lines, integrated service digital network lines, cable modem access or similar transfer mediums.

1.17 Any marginal note is for information purposes only and shall not be incorporated in or construed as part of the Policy.

1.18 Words in the singular include the plural and words in the plural include the singular

2 Basis of Contract

The Assured having made to Insurers a written proposal which together with any other related particulars and statements that have been supplied in writing are agreed to be incorporated herein and to form the basis of this Policy (it is also agreed that all such information supplied by any Assured shall be deemed to have been supplied by each and every Assured), and having paid to Insurers the premium stated in the Schedule, the Assured is indemnified subject to the Policy terms, conditions, limitations and exclusions for any claim made during the Period of Insurance arising only out of the exercise and conduct by or on behalf of the Assured of the Professional Business within the Geographical Limits.

3 Professional Liability

3.1 The Assured is indemnified against any claim made during the Period of Insurance for which the Assured shall become legally liable to pay compensation together with claimant's costs, fees and expenses in accordance with any judgment, award or settlement made within the Geographical Limits in consequence of:

3.1.1 Any breach of the professional duty of care owed by the Assured to the claimant which term is deemed to include a breach of warranty of authority.

3.1.2 Any libel, slander or slander of title, slander of goods or injurious falsehood.

3.1.3 The loss, destruction of or damage to any document in the care, custody and control of the Assured or for which the Assured is responsible (except to the extent insured by Section 4).

3.1.4 Any unintentional breach of copyright by the Assured or any employee of the Assured.

3.2 Costs Clause

In addition to the Limit of Indemnity the Insurers will pay defence costs provided that if a payment greater than the Limit of Indemnity available from Insurers has to be made to dispose of a claim, or if the Assured becomes under an obligation to pay a sum greater than the Limit of Indemnity as a result of a judgment, award, settlement or otherwise then Insurers' liability for defence costs associated with such claim shall be that proportion of the defence costs as the Limit of Indemnity available from Insurers for such claim bears to the amount required to be paid to dispose of the claim.

4 Additional Protection

The Assured is indemnified for reasonable and necessary costs and expenses first incurred during the Period of Insurance by the Assured arising out of the Professional Business in the United Kingdom and with the prior written consent of Insurers:

4.1 in replacing, restoring and reconstituting any document which is the property of the Assured or for which the Assured is responsible.

5 General Exclusions

The Policy shall not indemnify the Assured in respect of:

Excess

5.1 The Excess.

Consortium

5.2 Any claim arising out of the Professional Business carried out by the Assured for and/or in the name of any consortium or joint venture of which the Assured forms part unless specifically endorsed hereon.

Transport Property, etc.

5.3 Any claim arising out of the ownership, possession or use by or on behalf of the Assured of any aircraft, watercraft, hovercraft or motor vehicle or trailer, or any buildings, premises or land or that part of any building leased, occupied or rented by the Assured, or any property of the Assured.

Disclosed Circumstance

5.4 Any claim arising out of any circumstance or event which has been disclosed by the Assured to any insurer prior to the inception of this Policy.

Known Claims

5.5 Any claim or circumstance known or which reasonably should have been known to the Assured prior to inception of this Policy.

Employment

5.6 Any claim arising out of injury, disease, illness or death of the Assured or any person working under a contract of employment apprenticeship or service with the Assured, or any claim arising out of any dispute between the Assured and any present or former employee or any person who has been offered employment with the Assured.

Financial Services

5.7 Any claim arising directly or indirectly out of the provision of financial services regulated by the Financial Services Authority or the Personal Investment Authority or successor entity.

Trading Liability

5.8 Any claim arising out of or in connection with any trading loss or trading liability incurred by any business managed by or carried on by or on behalf of the Assured.

Fraud and Dishonesty

5.9 Any claim directly or indirectly contributed to or caused by any dishonest, fraudulent, criminal or malicious act or omission of any partner director or principal of the Assured.

Warranties, Penalties

5.10 Any claim arising out of any performance warranty (including but not limited to fitness for purpose warranties) guarantee, penalty clause or liquidated damages clause unless the liability of the Assured to the claimant would have existed in the absence of such warranty or clause.

Non-contribution

5.11 Any claim for which the Assured is or but for the existence of this Policy would be entitled to indemnity under any other insurance except in respect of any amount which exceeds that which would have been payable under such other insurance had this Policy not been effected.

Nuclear and War Risks

5.12 Liability for any claim:

5.12.1 directly or indirectly caused by or contributed to by or arising from (a) ionising radiations or contamination by radioactivity from any nuclear fuel or from any nuclear waste from the combustion of nuclear fuel, (b) the radioactive toxic explosive or other hazardous properties of any explosive nuclear assembly or nuclear component thereof;

5.12.2 directly or indirectly occasioned by or happening through or in consequence of war, invasion, acts of foreign enemies, hostilities (whether war be declared or not), civil war, rebellion, revolution, insurrection, military or usurped power.

Penal Damages

5.13.1 Any penal, punitive, exemplary or aggravated damages whenever identifiable as such.

5.13.2 Any additional damages under Section 97 (2) of the Copyright, Designs & Patents Act 1988 or any statutory successor to that Section.

5.13.3 Any fines or penalties of a criminal nature.

Territorial Limits

5.14 Any liability arising from Professional Business undertaken outside the Territorial Limits shown in the Schedule unless the project to which the Professional Business relates is to be constructed within the Territorial Limits.

Controlling Interest

5.15 Any claim made by:

(i) any party in which the Assured exercises a controlling interest by virtue of official position or shareholding; or

(ii) any party exercising a controlling interest over the Assured by virtue of it having a financial or executive interest in the operation of the Assured.

This Exclusion does not apply if the claim emanates from a wholly independent third party.

Binding Adjudications

5.16 Any claim arising from a contract which specifies the decision of an Adjudicator as finally determining any dispute unless the Insurers have given their prior written consent. However, this Exclusion shall not apply where the liability of the Assured would have existed in the absence of any such specification.

Cyber Liability Exclusion

5.17 Any claim or loss arising out of business conducted and/or transacted via the Internet, Intranet, Extranet, and/or via the Assured's own web-site, Internet site, web-address and/or via the transmission of electronic mail or documents by electronic means. For the avoidance of any doubt this Policy shall not indemnity the Assured in respect of any claim or loss arising out of any computer virus.

Where the liability to the Assured would have attached in the absence of the fact that the business is conducted and/or transacted via the Internet, Intranet, Extranet, and/or via the Assured's own web-site, Internet site, web-address and/or via the transmission of electronic mail or documents by electronic means, it is understood and agreed that the endorsement does not apply. It is understood and agreed that the onus of proof rests with the Assured and not with Insurers in this regard.

Supply of Goods

5.18 Any claim arising out of any goods or products sold, supplied, made, constructed, installed, maintained, repaired, altered or treated by or on behalf of the Assured unless any claim is a direct result of the Assured's negligent design and/or specification.

Director/Officer/Trustee

5.19 Any claim arising out of liability as a director, officer and/or trustee in their respective capacities.

Terrorism

5.20 Any loss, damage, cost or expense of whatsoever nature directly or indirectly caused by, resulting from or in connection with any act of terrorism regardless of any other cause or event contributing concurrently or in any other sequence to the loss.

For the purpose of this Exclusion an act of terrorism means an act, including but not limited to the use of force or violence and/or the threat thereof, of any person or group(s) of persons, whether acting alone or on behalf of or in connection with any organisation(s) or government(s), committed for political, religious, ideological or similar purposes including the intention to influence any government and/or to put the public, or any section of the public, in fear.

This Exclusion also excludes loss, damage, cost or expense of whatsoever nature directly or indirectly caused by, resulting from or in connection with any action taken in controlling, preventing, suppressing or in any way relating to any act of terrorism.

If Insurers allege that by reason of this Exclusion, any loss, damage, cost or expense is not covered by this Policy the burden of proving the contrary shall be upon the Assured.

6 General Conditions

Surveys

6.1 No indemnity is provided by Section 3.1.1 for claims arising out of any survey and/or valuation report carried out by or on behalf of the Assured unless the Assured has complied with the following conditions:

    6.1.1 the report is made in writing and;

    6.1.2 the survey and/or valuation is made by:

    6.1.2.1 a partner director or principal in the Firm or a member of the Assured's staff who is a Fellow or Professional Associate or Member of the Royal Institute of British Architects or of the Royal Institution of Chartered Surveyors or is a Registered Architect who has not less than one year's experience in undertaking structural surveys and/or valuation work such experience being related to the subject matter of the report or

    6.1.2.2 any member of the Assured's staff who has not less than five years' experience in undertaking structural surveys and/or valuation work such experience being related to the subject matter of the report and;

    6.1.3 except in the case where a report is provided to a Building Society, Insurance Company Bank or other such institutional lender upon a standard report form provided to the Assured for that purpose the Assured has incorporated in the report the following reservation:

> 'We have not inspected woodwork or other parts of the structure which are covered, unexposed or inaccessible and we are therefore unable to report that any such part of the property is free from defect.'

6.1.4 Where the Assured considers that High Alumina Cement may be present in a building the following paragraph is also to be added:

> 'Furthermore, we must stress that we have not carried out any investigation to determine whether High Alumina Cement was used during the construction of the building inspected and we are therefore unable to report that the building is free from risk in this respect. In view of the possible potential danger connected with High Alumina Cement we strongly recommend that the appropriate investigations, inspections and tests be carried out immediately by a suitable qualified engineer.'

6.1.5 any report and/or test made subsequent to the date of this Policy in connection with High Alumina Cement is carried out only by a suitably qualified engineer and presented in writing.

Notification Procedures

6.2 The Assured shall as a condition precedent to their right to be indemnified under:

6.2.1 Section 3 of this Policy, give notice in writing to Insurers as soon as possible during the Period of Insurance of any claim or of the receipt of notice from any person of an intention to make a claim and regardless of any previous notice, give notice in writing immediately on receipt of any Claim Form, Particulars of Claim, Arbitration Notice or any other formal document commencing legal proceedings of any kind.

6.2.2 Section 4.1 of this Policy, give notice in writing to Insurers as soon as possible during the Period of Insurance if during such Period of Insurance they shall discover that any document has been destroyed or damaged or lost or mislaid.

6.3 The Assured shall give during the Period of Insurance full details in writing as soon as possible of any circumstance or event of which the Assured shall first become aware during the Period of Insurance. Any such circumstance or event notified to Insurers during the Period of Insurance which subsequently gives rise to a claim shall be deemed to be a claim made during the Period of Insurance.

6.4 Receipt by the Assured of any 'Notice of Adjudication' and/or a 'referral notice' pursuant to the Scheme for Construction Contracts Regulations 1997 under the Housing Grants, Construction and Regeneration Act 1996 and/or any adjudication notice pursuant to contract must be notified immediately in writing to Fishburns, Solicitors, 61 St Mary Axe, London EC3A 8AA.

6.5 Notification of a 'notice of adjudication' and/or 'referral notice' and/or any adjudication notice pursuant to contract to Fishburns in writing will be considered as notification to Insurers. All other circumstances, claims and material facts must be notified to Insurers as per policy terms, conditions, limitations and exclusions.

6.6 It is agreed that Insurers shall be entitled to pursue legal, arbitration or other proceedings in the name of and on behalf of the Assured to challenge, appeal, open up or amend any decision, direction, award, or the exercise of any power of the Adjudicator or to stay the enforcement of any decision, direction, award or exercise of any power of the Adjudicator. The Assured shall give all such assistance as Insurers may reasonably require in relation to such proceedings. For the avoidance of doubt this section does not in any way limit Insurers' rights to subrogation.

6.7 Notice to Insurers to be given under this Policy shall be deemed to be properly made if received in writing by RIBA Insurance Agency Limited, at the address shown in the Schedule.

6.8 For the avoidance of doubt notice hereunder can *only* be made by the Assured (or agent of the Assured) and *not* by any other party).

Non-admission of Liability

6.9 The Assured shall not admit liability and no admission, arrangement, offer, promise or payment shall be made by the Assured without Insurers' written consent.

Insurers' Rights

6.10 Insurers shall be entitled, if they do desire, to take over and conduct in the name of the Assured the investigation representation defence or settlement of any claim circumstance or event and shall have full discretion in the conduct of the same. The Assured shall not be required to contest any legal proceedings unless a Queen's Counsel (or by mutual agreement between the Assured and the Insurers a similar authority) shall advise that such proceedings could be contested with the probability of success. It is a condition precedent to the Assured being indemnified by Insurers that the Assured shall give all such assistance as Insurers may reasonably require in the investigation representation defence or settlement of any claim circumstance or event.

6.11 In the event that Insurers shall be advised by their solicitors or on the advice of their solicitors' counsel that it is prudent to do so, Insurers shall be entitled to make a payment of the amount available from Insurers of the Limit of Indemnity or of an amount equivalent to that which any claim can be settled (whichever is the lesser) to the Assured in exoneration and total discharge of any further liability of any kind whatsoever by the Insurers to the Assured under this Policy. It shall be deemed to be proper payment in exoneration and discharge of the Insurers' liability hereunder to the Assured if the Insurers pay these monies to the RIBA Insurance Agency Limited.

6.12 Payment of the Excess by the Assured is a condition precedent to the Assured being indemnified by Insurers and the Assured shall confirm its ability and agreement to pay if reasonably requested by Insurers.

Applicable Law

6.13 This contract is governed by the laws of England. Any dispute or difference arising hereunder between the Assured and Insurers shall be referred to a Queen's Counsel of the English Bar to be mutually agreed between Insurers and the Assured or in the event of disagreement by the Chairman of the Bar Council. The Assured must give written notice within forty-five days of receipt of the Insurers' decision with which he is in dispute or difference.

Subrogation against Employees

6.14 Insurers shall not exercise any right of subrogation that may exist against any employee or former employee of the Assured unless Insurers shall have made a payment brought about or contributed to by the act or omission of the employee or former employee which was dishonest, fraudulent, criminal or malicious.

Additional Insurance

6.15 The Assured shall not effect insurance for any sum that exceeds the Limit of Indemnity without the prior written consent of the RIBA Insurance Agency Limited.

Fraud

6.16 If any request for indemnity is made and the same is false or fraudulent as regards the amount or otherwise this Policy shall become void and any indemnity hereunder shall be forfeited.

Pollution Limitation Clause

6.17 In consideration of the premium being paid by the Assured to the Insurers the Assured is indemnified in respect of any claims made and notified to the Insurers during the Period of Insurance arising out of pollution and/or contamination as a direct result of any breach of the professional duty of care owed by the Assured in connection with the Professional Business provided that the following additional Condition applies:

   The maximum amount payable in respect of all claims made under this endorsement shall not exceed in the aggregate the Limit of Indemnity specified in the Schedule including all costs and expenses incurred any such amount to be part of and not in addition to the Limit of Indemnity specified in the Schedule.

Cancellation

6.18 If the Assured becomes insolvent or bankrupt or a liquidator or Receiver is appointed or the Assured undertakes any act of bankruptcy, insolvency or liquidation this Insurance Contract is automatically cancelled with immediate effect unless Insurers shall in their absolute discretion agree otherwise in writing. If the Policy is cancelled the premium shall be payable on a pro rata basis for the period the Assured has been on risk.

Joint Insurance Contract

6.19 The Limit of Indemnity and the Excess applies to all Assureds jointly and for this purpose only this Policy is a joint Policy.

Rights of Third Parties

6.20 Notwithstanding the provisions of the Contracts (Rights of Third Parties) Act 1999, or otherwise, it is hereby agreed that:

   6.20.1 This Policy does not confer and does not purport to confer any rights upon any third party (whether or not an interest of any third party is noted in this Policy).

   6.20.2 The parties hereto shall be entitled to rescind or vary this Policy without the consent of any third party (whether or not any interest of any third party is noted in this policy).

   6.20.3 In the event of proceedings by a third party against the Insurer for the enforcement of a term of this Policy the Insurers shall have available to it by way of defence and set-off any matter which would have been available by way of defence and set-off if the proceedings had been brought by the Assured.

7 Special RIBA Conditions

7.1 Insurers will not exercise their right to avoid the Policy nor will Insurers reject a request for indemnity when it is alleged that there has been:

7.1.1 Non-disclosure of facts; or
7.1.2 Misrepresentation of facts; or
7.1.3 Incorrect particulars or statements; or
7.1.4 Late notification of a claim; or
7.1.5 Late notification of intention to make a claim; or
7.1.6 Late notification of a circumstance or event.

7.2 Provided this condition shall not apply to any claim known to the Assured prior to inception of this Policy.

7.3 Provided also that the Assured shall establish to Insurers' satisfaction that such alleged non-disclosure, misrepresentation or incorrect particulars or statements or late notice was innocent and free of any fraudulent conduct or intent to deceive.

7.4 When Insurers are so satisfied the following conditions shall apply:

7.4.1 Nothing in this clause shall entitle the Assured to indemnity wider or more extensive than is available to the Assured under this Policy (notwithstanding the terms of this clause).

7.4.2 Where the Assured's conduct or breach of or non-compliance with any condition of this Policy has resulted in prejudice to the handling or settlement of any claim, the indemnity afforded by this Policy in respect of such claim (including defence costs) shall be reduced to such sum as in Insurers' opinion would have been payable by them in the absence of such prejudice.

7.4.3 No indemnity shall be available for any claim, intention to make a claim, circumstance or event notified to Insurers after the Period of Insurance.

7.5 In the event of any disagreement by the Assured regarding the application of these Special Conditions, such disagreement shall at the Assured's request be referred to the person nominated by the President for the time being of the Royal Institute of British Architects for his consideration and intercession on the Assured's behalf if the facts are considered to warrant this by the person so nominated, and the Insurers agree to give due and proper consideration to any such intercession.

Appendix 2

APIA–RIBA Standard Form of Agreement for the Appointment of an Architect: Conditions of Engagement

Definitions

Where defined terms are used in SFA/99 they are distinguished by an initial capital letter.

Architect

The party referred to as Architect in the Agreement.

Brief

- At inception, the Client's initial statement of requirements;
- At the commencement of design (Work Stage C) the Client's requirements developed after consideration of any feasibility studies and set out by the Client in the Strategic Brief;
- After approval of the Detailed Proposals (Work Stage D) the detailed written Project Brief developed in conjunction with that design, unless and until varied by the Client.

CDM Regulations

The Construction (Design and Management) Regulations 1994.

Client

The party referred to as Client in the Agreement.

Construction Cost

The Construction Cost shall be the latest estimate for or the actual cost of constructing and/or managing the construction of the project, including:

- any contingency or design reserve cost allowance; and
- the cost as if new of any equipment provided or to be provided by the Client for installation under or in connection with any contract for which the Architect performs services.

The Construction Cost shall exclude:

- Value Added Tax;
- fees including design fees of any Specialists for work on which otherwise Consultants would have been employed. (*Where such fees are not known the Architect will estimate a reduction from the Construction Cost*);
- any loss and/or expense payments payable to, or liquidated damages recoverable from a contractor by the Client.

Consultant

A person, company or firm appointed by the Client to perform professional services in connection with the Project.

Effective Date

The date recorded in Article 6.

Planning Supervisor

As defined in the CDM Regulations.

Principal Contractor

As appointed, or to be appointed by the Client in accordance with CDM Regulations to carry out or manage work and perform duties in connection with the Project.

Project

As referred to in the Agreement.

Services

The Services to be performed by the Architect as specified in the Schedule of Services as may be varied by the Client from time to time.

Site

As specified in the Agreement.

Site Inspectors

Clerks of Works or others appointed by the Client to perform inspection services in connection with the construction of the Works.

Timetable

The period of time which the Client wishes to allow for the completion of the Services.

Third Party Agreement

An agreement between the Architect and a third party existing in parallel with the Agreement between the Architect and the Client.

Work Stages

Stages in to which the process of designing building projects and administering building contracts may be divided.

A Appraisal

Identification of Client's requirements and of possible constraints on development. Preparation of studies to enable the Client to decide whether to proceed and to select the probable procurement method.

B Strategic Briefing

Preparation of Strategic Brief by or on behalf of the Client confirming key requirements and constraints. Identification of procedures, organisational structure and range of Consultants and others to be engaged for the Project.

C Outline Proposals

Commence development of Strategic Brief into full Project Brief. Preparation of Outline Proposals and estimate of cost. Review of procurement route.

D Detailed Proposals

Complete development of the Project Brief. Preparation of Detailed Proposals. Application for full Development Control approval.

E Final Proposals

Preparation of final proposals for the Project sufficient for co-ordination and of all components and elements of the Project.

F Production Information

F1 Preparation of production information in sufficient detail to enable a tender or tenders to be obtained. Application for statutory approvals.
F2 Preparation of further production information required under the building contract.

G Tender Documentation

Preparation and collation of tender documentation in sufficient detail to enable a tender or tenders to be obtained for the construction of the Project.

H Tender Action

Identification and evaluation of potential contractors and/or Specialists for the Construction of the Project. Obtaining and appraising tenders and submission of recommendations to the Client.

J Mobilisation

Letting the building contract, appointing the Contractor, issuing of production information to the Contractor, and arranging site handover to the Contractor.

K   Construction to Practical Completion

Administration of the building contract up to and including practical completion. Provision to the Contractor of further information as and when reasonably required.

L   After Practical Completion

Administration of the building contract after practical completion. Making final inspections and settling the final account.

Works

Construction works for the Project to be carried out by a contractor or contractors.

Conditions

1   General

Interpretation

1.1 The headings and notes to these conditions are for convenience only and do not affect the interpretation of the conditions.
1.2 Words denoting the masculine gender include the feminine gender and words denoting natural persons include corporations and firms and shall be construed interchangeably in that manner.

Applicable law

1.3 The law applicable to this Agreement shall be that stated in the Appendix and, if not so stated, shall be the law of England and Wales.

Communications

1.4 Communications, between the Client and the Architect, including any notice or other document required under the Agreement, shall be in writing and given or served by any effective means. Communications that are not in writing shall be of no effect unless and until confirmed in writing by the sender or the other party. Communications shall take effect when received at an agreed address of the recipient. Communications sent by recorded or registered first-class post shall be presumed to have arrived at the address to which they are posted on the second day after posting.

Public Holidays

1.5 Where under this Agreement an action is required within a specific period of days, that period shall exclude any day which is a Public Holiday.

Services variation

1.6 In relation to the Services, either party shall advise the other upon becoming aware of:

  1 a need to vary the Services, the Timetable and/or the fees and/or any other part of the Agreement;

2 any incompatibility in or between any of the Client's requirements in the Brief; or between the Brief, any Client's instruction, the Construction Cost, the Timetable and/or the approved design; or any need to vary any part of them;
3 any issue affecting or likely to affect the progress, quality or cost of the Project;
4 any information or decision required from the Client or others in connection with performance of the Services.

and the parties shall agree how to deal with the matter.

2 Obligations and authority of the Architect

Duty of care

2.1 The Architect shall in performing the Services and discharging all the obligations under this Part 2 of these Conditions, exercise reasonable skill and care in conformity with the normal standards of the Architect's profession.

Architect's authority

2.2 The Architect shall act on behalf of the Client in the matters set out or necessarily implied in the Agreement.
2.3 In relation to the Services, the Architect shall obtain the authority of the Client before proceeding with the Services or initiating any Work Stage. The Architect shall confirm such authority in writing.

Appointment of Consultants or other persons

2.4 The Architect shall advise the Client on the appointment of Consultants or other persons, other than those named in Schedule 4 [*not reproduced here*], to design and/or carry out certain parts of the works or to provide specialist advice if required in connection with the Project.

Appointment of Site Inspectors

2.5 The Architect shall advise the Client on the appointment of full- or part-time Site Inspectors, other than those named in Schedule 4, under separate agreements where the Architect considers that the execution of the Works warrants such appointment.

Co-operation, etc.

2.6 The Architect in performing the Services shall when reasonably required by any of the persons identified in Schedule 4:

1 co-operate with them as reasonably necessary for carrying out their services;
2 provide them with information concerning the Services for carrying out their services;
3 consider and where appropriate comment on their work so that they may consider making any necessary changes to their work;
4 integrate into his work relevant information provided by them.

No alteration to Services or design

2.7 The Architect shall make no material alteration or addition to or omission from the Services or the approved design without the knowledge and consent of the Client, which consent shall be confirmed in writing by the Architect. In an emergency the Architect may make such alteration, addition or omission without the knowledge and consent of the Client but shall inform the Client without delay and subsequently confirm such action.

Visits to the Works

2.8 The Architect shall in providing the Services make such visits to the Works as the Architect at the date of the appointment reasonably expected to be necessary.

Obligations and authority of the Client

Client's representative

3.1 The Client shall name the person who shall exercise the powers of the Client under the Agreement and through whom all instructions shall be given.

Information, decisions, approvals and instructions

3.2 The Client shall supply, free of charge, accurate information as necessary for the proper and timely performance of the Services and to comply with CDM Regulation 11.
3.3 The Client, when requested by the Architect, shall give decisions and approvals as necessary for the proper and timely performance of the Services.
3.4 The Client shall advise the Architect of the relative priorities of the Brief, the Construction Cost and the Timetable.
3.5 The Client shall have authority to issue instructions to the Architect, subject to the Architect's right of reasonable objection. Such instructions and all instructions to any Consultants or Contractors or other persons providing services in connection with the Project shall be issued through the Lead Consultant.

Statutory and other consents required.

3.6 The Client shall instruct the making of applications for consents under planning legislation, building acts, regulations or other statutory requirements and by freeholders and others having an interest in the Project. The Client shall pay any statutory charges and any fees, expenses and disbursements in respect of such applications.

CDM Regulations

3.7 The Client shall, *where required by CDM Regulations*:

1 comply with his obligations under the CDM Regulations and in any conflict between the obligations under the Regulations and this Agreement, the former shall take precedence:
2 appoint a competent Planning Supervisor:
3 appoint a competent Principal Contractor.

Appointment and payment of others

3.8 Where it is agreed Consultants, or other persons, are to be appointed, the Client shall appoint and pay them under separate agreements and shall confirm in writing to the Architect the services to be performed by such persons so appointed.

Nominations

3.9 Either the Client or the Architect may propose the appointment of such Consultants or other persons, at any time, subject to acceptance by each party.

Site Inspectors

3.10 Where it is agreed Site Inspectors shall be appointed they shall be under the direction of the Lead Consultant and the Client shall appoint and pay them under separate agreements and shall confirm in writing to the Architect the services to be performed, their disciplines and the expected duration of their employment.

Responsibilities of others

3.11 The Client, in respect of any work or services in connection with the Project performed or to be performed by any person other than the Architect, shall:

1 hold such person responsible for the competence and performance of his services and for visits to the site in connection with the work undertaken by him;
2 ensure that such person shall co-operate with the Architect and provide to the Architect drawings and information reasonably needed for the proper and timely performance of the Services;
3 ensure that such person shall, when requested by the Architect, consider and comment on work of the Architect in relation to their own work so that the Architect may consider making any necessary change to his work.

3.12 The Client shall hold the Principal Contractor and/or other contractors appointed to undertake construction works and not the Architect responsible for their management and operational methods, for the proper carrying out and completion of the Works in compliance with the building contract and for health and safety provisions on the Site.

Legal advice

3.13 The Client shall procure such legal advice and provide such information and evidence as required for the resolution of any dispute between the Client and any other parties providing services in connection with the Project.

4 Assignment and sub-letting

Assignment

4.1 Neither the Architect nor the Client shall assign the whole or any part of the Agreement without the consent of the other in writing.

Sub-letting

4.2 The Architect shall not appoint any Sub-Consultants to perform any part of the Services without the consent of the Client, which consent shall not be unreasonably withheld. The Architect shall confirm such consent in writing.

5 Payment

Fees for performance of the Services

5.1 The Fees for performance of the Services, including the anticipated visits to the Works, shall be calculated and charged as set out in Schedule 3 [*not reproduced here*].

Work Stage fees shall be:

1 a percentage of the Construction Cost calculated in accordance with clause 5.2.2; or
2 lump sums in accordance with clause 5.3; or
3 time charges in accordance with clause 5.4; or
4 other agreed method.

Percentage fees

5.2

1 Percentage fees shall be in accordance with clause 5.2.2 or 5.3.1, as stated in Schedule 3.
2 Where this clause 5.2.2 is stated to apply in Schedule 3 the percentage or percentages stated therein shall be applied to the Construction Cost. Until the final Construction Cost has been ascertained interim fee calculations shall be based on:

(a) before tenders are obtained – the current approved estimate of the Construction Cost;
(b) after tenders have been obtained – the lowest acceptable tender;
(c) after the contract is let either the certified value or the anticipated final account.

The final fee shall be calculated on the ascertained gross final cost of all Works included in the Construction Cost, excluding any adjustment for loss and/or expense payable to or liquidated damages recoverable from a contractor by the Client.

Where the Client is the Contractor, the final cost shall include an allowance for the Contractor's profit and overheads.

Lump sums

5.3 A lump sum fee or fees shall be in accordance with clause 5.3.1 or 5.3.2 as stated in Schedule 3 and subject to clause 5.5. Such fee or fees shall be:

1 calculated by applying the percentages stated in Schedule 3, to be in accordance with this clause 5.3.1, to create:

(a) a lump sum or sums based on the Construction Cost approved by the Client at the end of Work Stage D: or

(b) separate lump sums for each Work Stage based on the Construction Cost approved by the Client at the end of the previous stage: or

2 a fixed lump sum or sums stated in Schedule 3 to be in accordance with this clause 5.3.2, which shall be adjusted in accordance with clause 5.6 if substantial amendments are made to the Brief and/or the Construction Cost and/or the Timetable.

Time charges

5.4 A time based fee shall be ascertained by multiplying the time reasonably spent in the performance of the Services by the relevant hourly rate set out in Schedule 3. Time 'reasonably spent' shall include the time spent in connection with performance of the Services in travelling from and returning to the Architect's office.

Revision of lump sums and time charge and other rates

5.5 Lump sums complying with clause 5.3.1a or 5.3.2, rates for time charges mileage and printing carried out in the Architect's office shall be revised every twelve months in accordance with changes in the Retail Price Index*. Each twelve-month period shall commence on the anniversary of the Effective Date of the Agreement, or the date of calculation of lump sums complying with clause 5.3.1a, whichever is the later.

Additional Fees

5.6 If the Architect, for reasons beyond his control is involved in extra work or incurs extra expense, for which he will not otherwise be remunerated, the Architect shall be entitled to additional fees calculated on a time basis unless otherwise agreed. Reasons for such entitlement include, but shall not be limited to:

1 the scope of the Services or the Timetable or the period specified for any work stage is varied by the Client;
2 the nature of the Project requires that substantial parts of the design can not be completed or must be specified provisionally or approximately before construction commences;
3 the Architects being required to vary any item of work commenced or completed pursuant to the Agreement or to provide a new design after the Client has authorised the Architect to develop an approved design;
4 delay or disruption by others;
5 prolongation of any building contract(s) relating to the Project;
6 the Architect consenting to enter into any third party agreement the form or beneficiary of which had not been agreed by the Architect at the date of the Agreement;
7 the cost of any work designed by the Architect or the cost of special equipment is excluded from the Construction Cost.

This clause 5.6 shall not apply where the extra work and/or expense to which it refers is due to a breach of the Agreement by the Architect.

---

* Retail Price Index is set out in Table 6.1 (All items) to 'Labour Market Trends' published by the Office for National Statistics.

Services not completed

5.7   Where for any reason the Architect provides only part of the Services specified in Schedule 2, the Architect shall be entitled to fees calculated as follows:

1   for completed Services, as described for those Services in Schedule 3;
2   for completed Work Stages, as apportioned for those Work Stages in Schedule 3.
3   for Services or Work Stages not completed, a fee proportionate to that described or apportioned in Schedule 3 based on the Architect's estimate of the percentage of completion.

Expenses and disbursements

5.8   The Client shall reimburse at net cost plus the handling charge stated in Schedule 3:

1   expenses specified in Schedule 3;
2   expenses other than those specified and incurred with the prior authorisation of the Client;
3   any disbursements made on the Client's behalf.

Maintain records

5.9   If the Architect is entitled to reimbursement of time spent on Services performed on a time basis, and of expenses and disbursements, the Architect shall maintain records and shall make these available to the Client on reasonable request.

Payment

5.10   Payments under the Agreement shall become due to the Architect on issue of the Architect's accounts. The final date for such payments by the Client shall be thirty days from the date of issue of an account.

The Architect's accounts shall be issued at intervals of not less than one month and shall include any additional fees, expenses or disbursement and state the basis of calculation of the amounts due.

Instalments of the fees shall be calculated on the basis of the Architect's estimate of the percentage of completion of the Work Stage or other Services or such other method specified in Schedule 3.

5.11   The Client may not withhold payment of any part of an account for a sum or sums due to the Architect under the Agreement by reason of claims or alleged claims against the Architect unless the amount to be withheld has been agreed by the Architect as due to the Client, or has been awarded in adjudication, arbitration or litigation in favour of the Client and arises out of or under the Agreement. Save as aforesaid, all rights of set-off at common law or in equity which the Client would otherwise be entitled to exercise are hereby expressly excluded.

Payment notices

5.12   A written notice from the Client to the Architect:

1   may be given within five days of the date of issue of an account specifying the amount the Client proposes to pay and the basis of calculation of that amount; and/or

2 shall be given, not later than five days before the final date for payment of any amount due to the Architect if the Client intends to withhold payment of any part of that amount stating the amount proposed to be withheld and the ground for doing so or, if there is more than one ground, each ground and the amount attributable to it.

If no such notices are given the amount due shall be the amount stated as due in the account. The Client shall not delay payment of any undisputed part of an account.

Late payment

5.13 Any sums due and remaining unpaid at the expiry of thirty days after the date of issue of an account from the Architect shall bear interest. Interest shall be payable at 8 per cent over Bank of England base rate current at the date of issue of the account.
5.14 For the avoidance of doubt the Architect's entitlement to interest at the expiry of thirty days after the date of issue of an account shall also apply to any amounts which an Adjudicator decides should be paid to the Architect.

Payment on suspension or determination

5.15 If the Client or the Architect suspends or determines performance of the Services, the Architect shall be entitled to payment of any part of the fee or other amounts due at the date of suspension or determination on issue of the Architect's account in accordance with clause 5.10.
5.16 Where the performance of the Services is suspended or determined by the Client, or suspended or determined by the Architect because of a breach of the Agreement by the Client, the Architect shall be entitled to payment of all expenses and other costs necessarily incurred as a result of any suspension and any resumption or determination on issue of the Architect's account in accordance with clause 5.10.

VAT

5.17 Fees, expenses and disbursements arising under the Agreement do not include Value Added Tax. The Client shall pay any Value Added Tax chargeable on the net value of the Architect's fees and expenses.

6 Copyright

Copyright

6.1 The Architect owns the copyright in the work produced by him in performing the Services and generally asserts the right to be identified as the author of the artistic work/work of architecture comprising the Project.

Licence

6.2 The Client shall have a licence to copy and use and allow other Consultants and Contractors providing services to the Project to use and copy drawings, documents and bespoke software produced by the Architect in performing the Services hereinafter called 'the Material', for purposes related to the Project on the Site or part of the Site to which the design relates.

Such purposes shall include its operation, maintenance, repair, reinstatement, alteration, extending, promotion, leasing and/or sale, but shall exclude the reproduction of the Architect's design for any part of any extension of the Project and/or for any other project unless a licence fee in respect of any identified part of the Architect's design is stated in Schedule 3.

Provided that:

1 the Architect shall not be liable if the Material is modified other than by or with the consent of the Architect, or used for any purpose other than that for which it was prepared, or used for any unauthorised purpose;
2 in the event of any permitted use occurring after the date of the last Service performed under the Agreement and prior to practical completion of the construction of the Project, the Client shall:

   (a) where the Architect has not completed Detailed Proposals (Work Stage D), obtain the Architect's consent, which consent shall not be unreasonably withheld; and/or
   (b) pay to the Architect a reasonable licence fee where no licence fee is specified in Schedule 3;

3 in the event of the Client being in default of payment of any fees or other amounts due, the Architect may suspend further use of the licence on giving seven days' notice of the intention of doing so. Use of the licence may be resumed on receipt of outstanding amounts.

7 Liabilities and insurance

Limitation of warranty by Architect

7.1 Subject always to the provisions of clause 2.1, the Architect does not warrant:

   1 that the Services will be completed in accordance with the Timetable;
   2 that planning permission and other statutory approvals will be granted;
   3 the performance, work or the products of others;
   4 the solvency of any other body appointed by the Client whether or not such appointment was made on the advice of the Architect.

Time limit for action or proceedings

7.2 No action or proceedings whatsoever for any breach of this Agreement or arising out of or in connection with this Agreement whether in contract, negligence, tort or howsoever shall be commenced against the Architect after the expiry of the period stated in the Appendix [*not reproduced here*] from the date of the last Services performed under the Agreement or (if earlier) practical completion of the construction of the Project.

Architect's liability

7.3 In any action or proceedings brought against the Architect under or in connection with the Agreement whether in contract, negligence, tort or howsoever the Architect's liability for loss or damage in respect of any one occurrence or series of occurrences arising out of one event shall be limited to whichever is the lesser of the sum:

1 stated in the Appendix; or
2 such sum as it is just and equitable for the Architect to pay having regard to the extent of his responsibility for the loss and/or damage in question when compared with the responsibilities of contractors, subcontractors, Consultants and other persons for that loss and/or damage. Such sum to be assessed on the basis that such persons are deemed to have provided contractual undertakings to the Client no less onerous than those of the Architect under the Agreement and had paid to the Client such sums as it would be just and equitable for them to pay having regard to the extent of their responsibility for that loss and/or damage.

Professional Indemnity Insurance

7.4 The Architect shall maintain Professional Indemnity Insurance cover in the amount stated in the Appendix for any one occurrence or series of occurrences arising out of any one event until at least the expiry of the period stated in the Appendix from the date of the last Services performed under the Agreement or (if earlier) practical completion of the construction of the Project provided such insurance is available at commercially reasonable rates and generally available in the insurance market to the Architect.

The Architect, when requested by the Client, shall produce for inspection documentary evidence that the Professional Indemnity Insurance required under the Agreement is being maintained.

The Architect shall inform the Client if such insurance ceases to be available at commercially reasonable rates in order that the Architect and Client can discuss the best means of protecting their respective positions in respect of the project in the absence of such insurance.

Third Party Agreements

7.5 Where the Client has notified, prior to the signing of this Agreement, that he will require the Architect to enter into an agreement with a third party or third parties and, the terms of which and the names or categories of other parties who will sign similar agreements are set out in an annex to this Agreement, then the Architect shall enter such agreement or agreements within a reasonable period of being requested to do so by the Client.

Rights of Third Parties

7.6 For the avoidance of doubt nothing in this Agreement shall confer or purport to confer on any third party any benefit or the right to enforce any term of this Agreement.

8 Suspension and determination

Suspension

8.1 The Client may suspend the performance of any or all of the Services by giving at least seven days' notice to the Architect. The notice shall specify the Services affected.
8.2 The Architect may suspend performance of the Services and his obligations under the Agreement on giving at least seven days' notice to the Client of his intention and the grounds for doing so in the event that the Client:

- is in default of any fees or other amounts due; or
- fails to comply with the requirements of the CDM Regulations.

The Architect shall resume performance of his obligations on receipt of the outstanding amounts.

8.3   If any period of suspension arising from a valid notice given under clause 8.1 or clause 8.2 exceeds six months the Architect shall request the Client to issue instructions. If written instructions have not been received within thirty days of the date of such request the Architect shall have the right to treat performance of any Service or his obligations affected as determined.

8.4   Any period of suspension arising from a valid notice given under clause 8.1 or clause 8.2 shall be disregarded in computing any contractual date for completion of the Services.

Determination

8.5   The Client or the Architect may by giving fourteen days' notice in writing to the other determine performance of any or all of the Services and the Architect's obligations under Part 2 of these Conditions stating the grounds for doing so and the Services and obligations affected.

8.6   Performance of the Services and the Architect's obligations under Part 2 of these Conditions may be determined immediately by notice from either party in the event of:

1   insolvency of the Client or the Architect; or
2   the Architect becoming unable to provide the Services through death or incapacity.

8.7   On determination of performance of the Services or the Architect's obligations under Part 2 of these Conditions, a copy of the Material referred to in clause 6.2 shall be delivered on demand to the Client by the Architect, subject to the terms of the licence under clause 6.2 and payment of the Architect's reasonable copying charges.

8.8   Determination of the performance of the Services or the Architect's obligations shall be without prejudice to the accrued rights and remedies of either party.

9 Dispute resolution*

Negotiation or conciliation

9.1   In the event of any dispute or difference arising under the Agreement, the Client and the Architect may attempt to settle such dispute or difference by negotiation or in accordance with the RIBA Conciliation Procedure.

Adjudication: England and Wales

9.2   Where the law of England and Wales is the applicable law, any dispute or difference arising out of this Agreement may be referred to adjudication by the Client or the Architect at any time. The adjudication procedures and the Agreement for the appointment of an Adjudicator shall be as set out in the 'Model Adjudication

---

* Architects are subject to the disciplinary sanction of the Architects Registration Board in relation to complaints of unacceptable professional conduct or serious professional incompetence.

Procedures' published by the *Construction Industry Council* current at the date of the reference. Clause 28 of the 'Model Adjudication Procedures' shall be deleted and replaced as follows: 'The Adjudicator may in his discretion direct the payment of legal costs and expenses of one party by another as part of his decision. The Adjudicator may determine the amount of costs to be paid or may delegate the task to an independent costs draftsman.'

Adjudication: Scotland

9.3

1 Where the law of Scotland is the applicable law, any dispute or difference touching or concerning any matter or thing arising out of this Agreement (other than with regard to the meaning or construction of this Agreement) may be referred to some independent and fit person within seven days of the application of the Client or the Architect and any fees which may become payable to the person so appointed shall be within the award of that person.
2 Any such Adjudicator appointed in terms of clause 9.3.1 hereof shall have twenty-eight days from the date of referral within which to reach a decision on the dispute, or such longer period as is agreed between the parties after the dispute has been referred but without prejudice, to the foregoing the Adjudicator shall be permitted to extend the said period of twenty-eight days by up to fourteen days, with the consent of the party by whom the dispute was referred.

The Adjudicator shall act impartially and shall be entitled to take the initiative in ascertaining the facts and the law relating be the dispute. The decision of the Adjudicator shall be binding on both parties until the dispute is finally determined by arbitration pursuant to clause 9.5 hereof.

The Adjudicator shall not be liable for anything done or omitted in the discharge or purported discharge of his functions as Adjudicator unless the act or omission is in bad faith, and all employees or agents of the Adjudicator are similarly protected from liability subject to the same proviso.

Naming or nomination of an Adjudicator

9.4 Where no Adjudicator is named and the parties are unable to agree on a person to act as Adjudicator, the Adjudicator shall be a person to be nominated at the request of either party by the nominator identified in the Appendix.

Arbitration

9.5 When in accordance with Article 5 either the Client or the Architect require any dispute or difference to be referred to arbitration the requiring party shall give notice to the other to such effect and the dispute or difference shall be referred to the arbitration and final decision of a person to be agreed between the parties or, failing agreement within fourteen days of the date of the notice, the appointor shall be the person identified in the Appendix.

Provided that where the law of England and Wales is applicable to the Agreement:

1 the Client or the Architect may litigate any claim for a pecuniary remedy which does not exceed £5,000 or such other sum as is provided by statute pursuant to section 91 of the Arbitration Act 1996:

2 the Client or the Architect may litigate the enforcement of any decision of an Adjudicator;
3 where and to the extent that the claimant in any dispute which is referred to arbitration is the Architect, the arbitrator shall not have the power referred to in Section 38(3) of the Arbitration Act 1996.

Costs

9.6 The Client shall indemnify the Architect in respect of his legal and other costs in any action or proceedings, together with a reasonable sum in respect of his time spent in connection with such action or proceedings or any part thereof.

1 the Architect obtains a judgment of the court or an Arbitrator's award in his favour for the recovery of fees and/or expenses under the Agreement; or
2 the Client fails to obtain a judgment of the court or an Arbitrator's award in the Client's favour for any claim or any part of any claim against the Architect.

Appendix 3
ACE Conditions of Engagement
Agreement A (1) 2002

B1 Definitions

The following definitions shall apply throughout this Agreement:

Additional Services

As so described in A 19.

Brief

A description of the requirements for the Project and the Works and for the relevant Services to be performed by the Consultant.

Client

As identified in the Memorandum of Agreement.

Client's Representative

The person designated by the Client under B3.5 and named as such in A9 [*not reproduced here*], or his replacement appointed in accordance with B3.5.

Consultant

As identified in the Memorandum Agreement.

Consultant's Intellectual Property Rights

Any and all Intellectual Property Rights created, developed, embodied in or in connection with any drawing, report, specification, bill of quantity, calculation or other document and information prepared by or on behalf of the Consultant in connection with the Project for delivery to the Client.

Contractor

A contractor appointed by the Client to execute or procure the execution of all or part of the Project or the Works and to co-ordinate and supervise or to procure the co-ordination and supervision of such execution.

Co-ordination Drawings

Drawings showing the inter-relationship of two or more engineering services and their relation to the structure and fabric of the Project or of the Works as the case may be.

Cost Plan

A document showing the estimated cost of all parts of the Project and how it is to be spent.

Individual

Any employee or member of the Consultant, including any officer or director of a company or a member of a limited liability partnership.

Insolvency

Either party becoming bankrupt, going into liquidation (either voluntarily or compulsory unless as part of a bona fide scheme of reconstruction or amalgamation), being dissolved, compounding with its creditors or having a receiver administrative receiver or administrator appointed of the whole or any part of its assets.

Intellectual Property Rights

All intellectual and industrial property rights including (without limitation) patents, trade marks, service marks, registered designs, copyrights, database rights, design rights, moral rights or know-how, howsoever arising, whether or not registered and any other similar protected rights in any country and any applications for the registration or protection of such rights and all extensions thereof throughout the world.

Lead Consultant

A person or firm appointed by the Client to co-ordinate the work of the Other Consultants.

Normal Services

As so described in A19.

Notice

A notice given in accordance with B10.

Other Consultants

Persons or firms other than the Consultant appointed or to be appointed by the Client to perform professional services in relation to the Project.

Project

As identified in the Memorandum of Agreement.

Project Cost

The total cost to the Client of the Project including:

(i) the total amounts paid or payable to the Contractor or Contractors responsible for managing and/or executing the Project and all its constituent parts;

(ii) the amounts of any liquidated damages or similar payments paid or payable by any Contractor or Contractors responsible for the execution of the Project;

(iii) a fair proportion of the total cost to the Client of any work in connection with the provision removal or diversion of any utilities systems associated with the Project which is carried out other than by any Contractor or Subcontractor, under arrangements made by the Consultant; the said fair proportion shall be assessed by the Consultant with reference to the costs incurred in making such arrangements;

(iv) the fair value of all labour materials goods plants and machinery (including the use of plant) provided by the Client for the Project;

(v) the cost of any investigations or tests in respect of the Project, whether carried out on site or elsewhere.

The Project Cost shall not include: administration expenses incurred by the Client; costs incurred by the Client under this Agreement or agreements with Other Consultants; interest on capital during construction and the cost of raising monies required for carrying out the construction of the Project; and the cost of land and wayleaves.

Project Leader

The person designated by the Consultant under B2.8 and named as such in A8, or his replacement appointed in accordance with B2.8.

Services

The totality of Normal Services and Additional Services.

Site Staff

Any person or persons appointed under B4 including any staff of the Consultant seconded to Site or premises outside the Consultant's offices on work in connection with the Works on a full time or part time basis.

Stages

The stages for the performance of the Services as described in the Schedule of Services.

Sub-contractor

A person or firm appointed by or on behalf of a Contractor to execute part of the Project or of the Works or to manufacture or supply material for incorporation therein.

Tender Documentation

Drawings and other documentation as appropriate to the agreed procurement method prepared to enable those tendering to interpret the design for the Project and to submit a tender for executing all or any part of the Project.

Works

As so described in A7.

Works Cost

The total cost to the Client of the Works including:

(i) the total amounts paid or payable to the Contractor or Contractors responsible for managing and/or executing the Works and all its constituent parts including associated builders' work, attendance and profit and the cost of the preliminary and general items in the proportion that the Works Cost bears to the Project Cost;

(ii) the amounts of any liquidated damages or similar payments paid or payable by any Contractor or Contractors responsible for the execution of the Works;

(iii) a fair proportion of the total cost to the Client of any work in connection with the provision removal or diversion of any utilities systems associated with the Works which is carried out other than by any Contractor or Subcontractor, under arrangements made by the Consultant; the said fair proportion shall be assessed with reference to the costs incurred by the Consultant in making such arrangements;

(iv) the fair value of all labour materials goods plant and machinery (including the use of plant) provided by the Client for the Works;

(v) the cost of any investigations or tests in respect of the Works whether carried out on site or elsewhere.

The Works Cost shall not include: administration expenses incurred by the Client; costs incurred by the Client under this Agreement or agreements with Other Consultants; interest on capital during construction and the cost of raising monies required for carrying out the construction of the Works; and the cost of land and wayleaves.

B2   Obligations of the consultant

Headings are explanatory and do not form part of the Conditions.

Normal Services

2.1 The Consultant shall perform the Normal Services.

Additional Services

2.2 The Consultant shall perform such Additional Services as may be requested or consented to by the Client.

Skill and Care

2.3 The Consultant shall exercise reasonable skill, care and diligence in the performance of the Services.

Assignment

2.4 The Consultant shall not, without written consent of the Client which consent shall not unreasonably be delayed or withheld, assign or transfer any benefit or obligation under this Agreement.

Other Consultants

2.5 The Consultant shall if so requested advise the Client on the need for and the selection and appointment of Other Consultants to perform services in respect of the Project. The Consultant acting as Lead Consultant shall co-ordinate and integrate the services of such Other Consultants as the Client may appoint. The Consultant shall not be responsible for the detailed designs of any Other Consultant or liable for defects in or omissions from them.

Specialist Sub-consultants

2.6 The Consultant may recommend to the Client that the Consultant sub-lets to a specialist sub-consultant the performance of any of the Services. The Client shall not unreasonably withhold consent to such recommendation and the Consultant shall integrate such sub-consultant's services with his own. The Consultant shall be responsible for the performance and the payment of any sub-consultant.

Design by Contractors or Sub-contractors

2.7 The Consultant may recommend to the Client that the detailed design of any part of the Works should be carried out by a Contractor or Sub-contractor and the Client shall not unreasonably withhold consent to such recommendation. The Consultant shall examine in accordance with C8.2 that detailed design and integrate it into his own design. The Consultant shall not be responsible for such detailed design or liable for defects in or omissions from it.

Project Leader

2.8 The Consultant shall designate a Project Leader who shall be deemed to have authority to make decisions on behalf of the Consultant under this Agreement. The Project Leader shall not be replaced without the consent of the Client, which consent shall not unreasonably be delayed or withheld.

Timeliness

2.9 All requests to the Client by the Consultant for information, assistance or decisions required in accordance with B3.1, B3.2 and B3.3 shall be made in a timely fashion. Subject always to conditions beyond his reasonable control, (including acts or omissions of the Client or third parties) the Consultant shall use reasonable endeavours to perform the Services in accordance with any programme agreed with the Consultant from time to time.

Authority

2.10 The Consultant shall not without further approval of the Client alter the design once approved by the Client. Save in the event of any emergency, the Consultant shall not without the approval of the Client issue instructions to any Contractor the effect of which would be to alter any design already approved by the Client or to incur additional costs to the Client beyond whatever limits may have been agreed for such additional costs.

Consultant's Discretion

2.11 If in the performance of the Services the Consultant has a discretion exercisable as between the Client and a Contractor or Subcontractor the Consultant shall exercise that discretion fairly.

B3 Obligations of the client

Information needed by the Consultant

3.1 The Client shall supply to the Consultant, without charge and in such time so as not to delay or disrupt the performance by the Consultant of the Services, all necessary and relevant data and information (including details of the services to be performed by any Other Consultants) in the possession of the Client, his agents, servants, Other Consultants or Contractors.

Assistance

3.2 The Client shall give, and shall procure that his agents, servants, Other Consultants and Contractors give, such assistance as shall reasonably be required by the Consultant in the performance of the Services.

Decisions

3.3 The Client shall ensure that his decisions, instructions, consents or approvals on or to all matters properly referred to him shall be given in such reasonable time so as not to delay or disrupt the performance of the Services by the Consultant.

Assignment

3.4 The Client shall not, without the written consent of the Consultant which consent shall not unreasonably be delayed or withheld, assign or transfer any benefit or obligation under this Agreement.

Client's Representative

3.5 The Client shall designate a Client's Representative who shall be deemed to have authority to make decisions on behalf of the Client under this Agreement. The Client shall notify the Consultant immediately if the Client's Representative is replaced.

Contractors

3.6 The Client shall appoint Contractors to execute and/or to manage the execution of the Project and the Works. The Client shall require that the Contractors execute the Project and the Works in accordance with the terms of the relevant contracts. Neither the provision of Site Staff nor periodic visits by the Consultant or his staff to the site shall in any way affect the responsibilities of the Contractors or any Subcontractors for constructing the Project and the Works in compliance with the relevant contract documents and any instructions issued by the Consultant.

B4 Site staff

Provision of Site Staff

4.1 If in the opinion of the Consultant the execution of the Works including any geotechnical investigations warrants full time or part time Site Staff to be deployed at any stage the Client shall not unreasonably withhold consent to the employment and/or deployment of such reasonably qualified technical and clerical Site Staff as the Consultant shall consider necessary. The Client and the Consultant shall discuss, agree and confirm in writing in advance of such deployment the number and levels of staff to be deployed to site, the duration of such deployments, the frequency of occasional visits and the duties to be performed by Site Staff.

Terms of Employment of Site Staff

4.2 Site Staff shall be employed either by the Consultant or by the Client directly. The terms of service of all Site Staff to be employed by the Consultant shall be subject to the approval of the Client, which approval shall not unreasonably be delayed or withheld.

Instructions to Site Staff

4.3 The Client shall procure that the contracts of employment of Site Staff employed by the Client empower the Consultant to issue instructions to such staff in relation to the Works and shall stipulate that staff so employed shall in no circumstances take or act upon instructions in connection with the Works other than those given by the Consultant.

Responsibility for Site Staff

4.4 Where duties are performed by Site Staff employed other than by the Consultant, the Consultant shall not be responsible for any failure on the part of such staff properly to comply with any instructions given by the Consultant.

Facilities and Arrangements for Site Staff

4.5 The Client shall be responsible for the cost and provision of such local office accommodation, furniture, telephones and facsimile apparatus and other office equipment, protective clothing and transport on site as shall reasonably be required for the use of Site Staff and for the reasonable running costs of such necessary local office accommodation and other facilities, including those of stationery, telephone and facsimile charges, and postage. Unless agreed between the Client and the Consultant that the Client shall arrange for such facilities, the Consultant shall arrange, whether through Contractors or otherwise, for the provision of such local office accommodation and other facilities.

B5 Commencement, termination, suspension, disruption and delay

Duration of Appointment

5.1 Notwithstanding the date stated in the Memorandum of Agreement, the effective date of the appointment of the Consultant shall be the date upon which the Memorandum of Agreement was executed by the parties or the date when the Consultant shall have first commenced performance of the Services, whichever is the earlier. Unless terminated, the appointment of the Consultant shall be concluded when the Consultant has performed the Services required under this Agreement.

Termination by the Client

5.2 The Client may terminate the appointment of the Consultant at any time by Notice in respect of all or any part of the Services.

Termination by the Consultant in Certain Circumstances

5.3 If circumstances arise for which the Consultant is not responsible and which he considers make it irresponsible for him to perform all or any part of the Services the Consultant shall be entitled to terminate his appointment by two weeks' Notice in respect of all or such part of the Services.

Suspension by the Client

5.4 The Client may at any time by Notice require the Consultant to suspend the performance of all or any part of the Services. On Notice of suspension of all or any part of the Services the Consultant shall cease such suspended Services in an orderly and economical manner compatible with a possible order to restart. If the suspension of the performance of all or any part of the Services exceeds twelve months in aggregate the Consultant may by giving four weeks' Notice treat the Project or the Works or that part of the Project or the Works as having been abandoned and the appointment of the Consultant in respect of all or any part of the Services affected shall be automatically terminated.

Termination by the Client following a Breach of this Agreement by the Consultant

5.5 In the event of a breach of this Agreement by the Consultant the Client may give two weeks' Notice of his intention to terminate the appointment of the Consultant setting out the acts or omissions of the Consultant relied upon as evidence of such breach. If the Consultant does not, to the reasonable satisfaction of the Client, take expeditious steps to repair the breach during the notice period the Client may forthwith on the expiry of the notice period terminate the appointment of the Consultant by a further Notice.

Suspension by the Consultant

5.6 Upon the occurrence of any circumstance beyond the control of the Consultant which is such as to prevent or significantly impede the performance by the Consultant of the Services under this Agreement, the Consultant may without prejudice to any other remedy and upon not less than four weeks' Notice suspend for a period of up to twenty-six weeks the performance of the Services under this Agreement in respect of all or such parts of the Project or the Works as are affected and at the expiry of the said period of suspension either continue with the performance of the Services under this Agreement or if he is still prevented from performing such Services for reasons beyond his control terminate his appointment forthwith by a further Notice in respect of all or any part of the Services affected.

Termination by the Consultant following a Breach of this Agreement by the Client

5.7 In the event of a breach of this Agreement by the Client the Consultant may give two weeks' Notice of his intention to terminate the appointment of the Consultant setting out the acts or omissions of the Client relied upon as evidence of such breach. If the Client does not, to the reasonable satisfaction of the Consultant, take expeditious steps to repair the breach during the notice period the Consultant may forthwith on the expiry of the notice period terminate the appointment of the Consultant by a further Notice. Notwithstanding the foregoing, in the event of the failure of the Client to make any payment properly due to the Consultant in accordance with the provisions of B6 by the final date for payment the Consultant may, upon not less than two weeks' Notice, terminate his appointment.

Insolvency

5.8 The appointment of the Consultant may be terminated in the event of Insolvency of either party. Notice of termination must be given to the party which is insolvent by the other party.

Accrued Rights

5.9 Termination of the Consultant's appointment under this Agreement shall not prejudice or affect the accrued rights or claims of either party to this Agreement.

B6 Payment

Payment of Fees and Expenses

6.1 Payment by the Client to the Consultant for the performance of the Services shall comprise fees and if so agreed expenses.

Fees

6.2

Normal Services

6.2.1 Fees for the performance of the Normal Services shall be paid in accordance with these Conditions and A20.1 and A21.

Additional Services

6.2.2 Fees for the performance of Additional Services if any shall unless otherwise agreed be time based and paid in accordance with these Conditions and A20.2 and A21.1, save that the instalments shall start at the next instalment date provided by A21.1. If a lump sum fee has been agreed, it shall be paid in accordance with A21.2.

Services performed by Others

6.2.3 Where the Consultant has arranged for the performance by others on behalf of the Client of any of the services specified in C11, the Client shall pay direct to such person or persons their fees and expenses for performing such services. The Consultant shall obtain the prior agreement of the Client to the arrangements which he proposes to make as agent for the Client for the performance by others of any services specified in C11.

Time Based Fees

6.2.4 Where time based fees are to be paid, they shall be at the rates set out in A20.2 and calculated by multiplying the hourly or daily rates applicable to the persons concerned by the number of hours or days (as the case may be) spent by such persons in performing the Services, including time spent in travelling in connection with the Project or the Works. Payment shall be by instalments in accordance with A21.1.

Lump Sum Fees

6.2.5 Where lump sum fees are to be paid, they shall be as set out in A20.1 with payment by instalments in accordance with A21.3.

Percentage Fees

6.2.6 Where payment is to be based on the final Works Cost/Project Cost, the fee shall be the percentage of the final Works Cost/Project Cost set out in A20.1 with payment by instalments in accordance with A21.3. Where payment is to be based on estimates of the Works Cost/Project Cost made at the completion of each Stage, the fees for each Stage shall be calculated as set out in A20.1 with payment by instalments in accordance with A21.3.

Expenses

6.3 Unless included in the fees, the Client shall pay the Consultant's expenses incurred in performing the Services in accordance with A22. Unless otherwise agreed, expenses shall comprise those payments reasonably and properly made by the Consultant for:

(i) printing, reproduction and purchase of documents, maps, records and photographs;
(ii) courier charges;
(iii) travelling, hotel expenses and subsistence payments;
(iv) any other expenses for which repayment is authorised.

Site Staff

6.4 In addition to any other payment to be made under this Agreement, the Client shall pay the Consultant for all Site Staff employed by the Consultant. Unless otherwise agreed, payment for Site Staff shall be on a time basis and at the rates set out in A20.2 with instalments in accordance with A21.1, save that the instalments shall start at the next instalment date provided by A21.1.

Local Authority Charges

6.5 Notwithstanding anything to the contrary contained in this Agreement, the Client shall pay the Consultant for any fees, costs or charges paid by the Consultant to local or other authorities for seeking and obtaining statutory permissions.

Time for Payment

6.6

Due Date and Final Date

6.6.1 Payments due to the Consultant under this Agreement shall become due for payment on submission of the Consultant's invoice therefor and the final date for payment shall be 28 days thereafter. Interest shall be added to all amounts remaining unpaid thereafter as set out in A23.

Notice of Payment

6.6.2 The Client shall not later than five days after the date on which a payment becomes due from him under this Agreement or would have become due if:

(i) the Consultant had carried out his obligations under this Agreement, and
(ii) no set off or abatement was permitted by reference to any sum claimed to be due under one or more other contracts

give a Notice specifying the amount (if any) of the payment made or proposed to be made and the basis on which that amount was calculated.

Notice of Withholding

6.6.3 The Client may not withhold any payment after the final date for payment of any sum due under this Agreement unless he gives, not later than seven days before such final date, a Notice specifying the amount proposed to be withheld and the ground for withholding payment or if there is more than one ground, each ground and the amount attributable to it.

Variation or Disruption of Consultant's Work

6.7 If the Consultant has to carry out additional work and/or suffers disruption in the performance of the Services because:

(i) the Project or the Works or Brief is or are varied by the Client; or
(ii) of any delay by the Client in fulfilling his obligation or in taking any other step necessary for the execution of the Project or the Works; or
(iii) the Consultant is delayed by others (or by events which were not reasonably foreseeable); or
(iv) the Project or the Works is damaged or destroyed; or
(v) of other reasons beyond the control of the Consultant

the Client shall make an additional payment to the Consultant in respect of the additional work carried out and additional resources employed (unless and to the extent that the additional work has been occasioned by the failure of the Consultant to exercise reasonable skill, care and diligence) and/or the disruption suffered. The additional payment shall be calculated (unless otherwise agreed) on the basis of time based fees as set out in A20.2 with payment by instalments in accordance with A21.1 save that instalments shall start at the next instalment date provided by A21.1. The Consultant shall advise the Client when he becomes aware that any such additional work shall be required or disruption shall be suffered and shall if so requested by the Client give an initial estimate of the additional payment likely to be incurred. Where the Client requires that payment for such additional work or disruption is to be in the form of lump sums, these lump sums and the intervals at which instalments shall be paid and the amounts of each instalment should be agreed prior to the additional work being commenced. For the avoidance of doubt it is hereby agreed that if the Consultant carries out any work which subsequently becomes redundant the Client shall (unless otherwise agreed) pay the Consultant therefor on the basis of time based fees as herein set out.

Effect of Termination or Suspension

6.8 In the event of any termination or suspension by the Client or the Consultant in accordance with B5 other than termination by the Client following breach of this Agreement by the Consultant or Insolvency of either party the Client shall pay the Consultant a fair and reasonable amount on account of the fees due under B6 commensurate with the Services performed to the date of such termination or suspension and any outstanding expenses together with a sum for loss and costs of disruption (calculated on the basis of the loss to the Consultant and costs to which the Consultant is committed in respect of planned future work on the Project or the Works). In the event of any termination by the Client following breach of this Agreement by the Consultant or Insolvency of either party in accordance with B5 the Client shall pay the Consultant a fair and reasonable amount on account of the fees due under B6 commensurate with the Services performed to the date of termination and any outstanding expenses.

Further Payments

6.9 Further payments due to the Consultant in accordance with B6.4, B6.5, B6.7 and B6.8 shall be invoiced with the next account to be presented by the Consultant.

VAT

6.10 All sums due under this Agreement are exclusive of Value Added Tax, the amount of which shall be paid by the Client to the Consultant at the rate and in the manner prescribed by law.

B7 Intellectual property and confidentiality

Consultant's Intellectual Property Rights

7.1 The Consultant's Intellectual Property Rights shall, as the case may be, vest in or remain vested in the Consultant but the Client shall have a licence to use the Consultant's Intellectual Property Rights for any purpose related to the Project. Such licence shall enable the Client to use such Consultant's Intellectual Property Rights for the extension of the Project but such use shall not include a licence to reproduce the designs contained therein for any extension of the Project. In the event of the Client being in default of payment of any fees or other amounts due under this Agreement the Consultant may revoke the licence granted herein on giving seven days' Notice. Save as above, the Client shall not make copies of any of the Consultant's drawings or other documents or information, nor shall he use any of the Consultant's Intellectual Property Rights in connection with any other works without the prior written approval of the Consultant which shall not unreasonably be withheld and upon such terms as may be agreed between the Client and the Consultant. The Consultant shall not be liable for the use by any person of any of the Consultant's Intellectual Property Rights for any purpose other than that for which the same were prepared by or on behalf of the Consultant.

Publication and Confidentiality

7.2 The Consultant shall not, without written consent of the Client, publish alone or in conjunction with any other person any articles, photographs or other illustrations relating to the Project. Neither party shall disclose to any other person any private or confidential information unless so authorised by the other party save in the proper course of his duties or as required or permitted by law.

B8 Liability, insurance and warranties

Limitation of Liability

8.1 Notwithstanding anything to the contrary contained in this Agreement, the liability of the Consultant under or in connection with this Agreement whether in contract or in tort, in negligence, for breach of statutory duty or otherwise (other than in respect of personal injury or death) shall not exceed the sum or sums recoverable under A10.

Net Contribution

8.2 Subject to B8.1 but notwithstanding otherwise anything to the contrary contained in this Agreement, such liability of the Consultant for any claim or claims shall be further limited to such sum as it would be just and equitable for the Consultant to pay having regard to the extent of his responsibility for the loss or damage suffered as a result of the occurrence or series of occurrences in question ('the loss and damage') and on the assumptions that:

   (i) all Other Consultants and all Contractors and Subcontractors shall have provided contractual undertakings on terms no less onerous than those set out in B2.3 to the Client in respect of the carrying out of their obligations;
  (ii) there are no exclusions of or limitations of liability nor joint insurance or co-insurance provisions between the Client and any other party referred to in this clause and any such other party who is responsible to any extent for the loss and damage is contractually liable to the Client for the loss and damage; and
 (iii) all Other Consultants and all Contractors and Subcontractors have paid to the Client such proportion of the loss and damage which it would be just and equitable for them to pay having regard to the extent of their responsibility for the loss and damage.

Liability of Employees

8.3 Save in respect of death or personal injury the Client shall look only to the Consultant (and not to any Individual) for redress if the Client considers that there has been any breach of this Agreement. The Client agrees not to pursue any claims in contract tort or statute (including negligence) against any Individual as a result of carrying out its obligations under or in connection with this Agreement at any time and whether named expressly in this Agreement or not.

Limitation of Time within which to bring Claims

8.4 No action or proceedings under or in respect of this Agreement whether in contract or in tort or in negligence or for breach of statutory duty or otherwise shall be commenced against the Consultant after the expiry of the period of liability stated in A11 or such earlier date as may be prescribed by law.

Professional Indemnity Insurance

8.5 The Consultant shall maintain professional indemnity insurance in an amount not less than that stated in A12 for any one occurrence or series of occurrences arising out of this Agreement and for the period stated in A13, provided that within that amount any annual aggregate stated in the relevant insurance policy in respect of claims for pollution and contamination shall not be less than the amount stated therefor in A14, and provided always that such insurance is available at commercially reasonable rates. The Consultant shall immediately inform the Client if such insurance ceases to be available on the terms required by this Condition at commercially reasonable rates in order that the Client and the Consultant can discuss means of best protecting their respective positions in the absence of such insurance.

Public Liability Insurance

8.6 The Consultant shall maintain public liability insurance covering the Consultant, his employees, agents and in respect of the acts of sub-consultants from the effective date of this Agreement until the completion of the Services in the sum stated in A15, provided always that such insurance is available at commercially reasonable rates.

Insurance Documentation

8.7 As and when reasonably requested to do so by the Client, the Consultant shall produce for inspection brokers' certificates to show that the insurance cover required under B8.5 and B8.6 is being maintained.

Collateral Warranties

8.8 When the Client and the Consultant have so agreed before the commencement of the appointment, the Consultant shall enter into and provide collateral warranties for the benefit of other parties. It shall be a condition of the provision of such warranties that they shall give no greater benefit to those to whom they are issued in quantum, duration or otherwise than is given to the Client under the terms of this Agreement. Should the Client request alterations to the previously agreed terms or the execution of warranties in addition to those previously agreed, and the Consultant consents to such a request, these may be entered into and provided by the Consultant for such additional fee or other consideration as the parties may agree.

B9 Disputes and differences

Mediation

9.1 The parties shall attempt in good faith to settle any dispute by mediation.

Adjudication

9.2 Where this Agreement is a construction contract within the meaning of the Housing Grants, Construction and Regeneration Act 1996 either party may refer any dispute arising under this Agreement to adjudication in accordance with the Construction Industry Council Model Adjudication Procedure.

B10 Notices

10.1 Any Notice to be given under this Agreement shall be in writing and given by sending the same by fax or by first class letter to the Client or the Consultant at the appropriate address as shown on the Memorandum of Agreement. Notices shall take effect when they have been received by the Client or the Consultant as the case may be.

Appendix 4

RICS Form of Agreement and Terms and Conditions of the Appointment of a Quantity Surveyor, 1992

Form of Agreement

THIS AGREEMENT is made the _____ day of _____ year

BETWEEN _____ ('the Client')

of _____

_____

and _____

_____ ('the Quantity Surveyor')

of _____

_____

The Client intends to proceed with _____

_____

_____ ('the project')

at _____

_____ ('the site')

This Agreement relates to and shall be deemed to include the whole of the Form of Enquiry, Schedule of Services and Fee Offer, applicable to the project as so certified by the parties to this Agreement, together with the attached Terms of Appointment.

The Client hereby appoints the Quantity Surveyor in respect of the project to provide the services specified in the Schedule of Services and the Quantity Surveyor agrees to provide them.

The law in _____ and the jurisdiction of

the Courts in _____ apply to this Agreement

IN WITNESS whereof this Agreement was executed as a Deed and delivered the day and year first before written [*1]

by the Quantity Surveyor _____

by the Client _____

AS WITNESS the hands of the parties the day and year first before written [*2]

Signed by or on behalf of the Quantity Surveyor _____

Signed by or on behalf of the Client _____

Note: *1 and *2 are alternatives – delete as appropriate.
*1 is for use when the Agreement is to be executed as a Deed.
*2 is for use when the Agreement is to be executed under hand.

Terms of Appointment

1 *Introduction*

1.1 The Quantity Surveyor shall provide the services with reasonable skill, care and diligence.

2 *Client's obligations*

2.1 The Client shall supply such information to the Quantity Surveyor at such times as is reasonably required for the performance of the services.
2.2 The Client shall notify the Quantity Surveyor in writing of any agent appointed to act on behalf of the Client and of any change or dismissal of the agent.
2.3 The Client shall notify the Quantity Surveyor in writing of any instruction to vary the services.

3 *Assignment and subcontracting*

3.1 Neither the Client nor the Quantity Surveyor shall assign the whole or any part of this Agreement without the consent of the other in writing. Such consent shall not be unreasonably withheld.
3.2 The Quantity Surveyor shall not subcontract any part of the services without the consent of the Client in writing.

4 *Payment*

4.1 The Client shall pay the Quantity Surveyor for the performance of the services the fees and charges in such instalments as are set out in Clause 4 of the Fee Offer. All fees and charges under the Agreement are exclusive of Value Added Tax which if due shall be paid concurrently in addition. The 'due date for payment' shall be seven days (see Clause 14.3 below) after the date of the submission of the invoice. The Quantity Surveyor when submitting his invoice shall on each invoice confirm the basis on which the stated amount is calculated.
4.2 The 'final date for payment' shall be twenty-one days after the due date for payment. Payment shall be made no later than the final date for payment.
4.3 The Client must, not later than five days after the due date for payment, give to the Quantity Surveyor written notice stating the amount which the Client

proposes to pay and the basis on which that amount is calculated. Where no such notice is given the amount to be paid is that stated in the invoice.

4.4 Where the Client intends to withhold payment of any amount either stated in the Quantity Surveyor's invoice or in a written notice given by the Client under Clause 4.3 above, the Client must give written notice to the Quantity Surveyor not later than five days before the final date for payment, stating the amount to be withheld and the grounds for withholding payment.

4.5 Any amounts due to the Quantity Surveyor under this Agreement which remain unpaid by the Client after the final date for payment shall bear interest at the rate stated in Clause 5 of the Fee Offer.

4.6 In the event that the Client is in default over payment of amounts at the final date for payment and no notice of intention to withhold payment from such amount has been given under Clause 4.4 above, the Quantity Surveyor may suspend performance of any or all of the services. This right is subject to the Quantity Surveyor first giving the Client not less than seven days' written notice of such intention and stating the grounds for suspension. The right to suspend performance shall cease when the Client makes payment of the amount due. Any such period of suspension shall be disregarded for the purposes of contractual time limits previously agreed for the completion of the services. Such suspension shall not be treated as a suspension under Clause 8 below.

4.7 The Quantity Surveyor shall notify the Client in writing as soon as it becomes reasonably apparent that any work additional to the subject of this Agreement will be required.

4.8 Where the Quantity Surveyor is involved in additional work because of:

- changes in the scope of the works, and/or
- changes in the programme of the works, and/or
- changes instructed to the services, and/or
- the commencement of adjudication, arbitration or litigation

the Client shall pay to the Quantity Surveyor additional fees calculated (unless otherwise agreed) on the time charge basis in Clause 2 of the Fee Offer.

5 Professional indemnity insurance

5.1 The Quantity Surveyor is required to comply with the regulations of the Royal Institution of Chartered Surveyors in respect of the maintenance of professional indemnity insurance. He shall use reasonable endeavours to take out and maintain such professional indemnity insurance above RICS limits, provided that it is available at commercially reasonable rates, as defined by reference to an amount and for a period in Clause 8 of the Form of Enquiry. Such insurance shall be with an insurer who is listed for this purpose by the RICS.

5.2 The Quantity Surveyor shall on the written request of the Client provide evidence that the insurance is properly maintained.

5.3 The Quantity Surveyor shall immediately inform the Client if the insurance referred to in Clause 5.1 above ceases to be available at commercially reasonable rates in order that the best means of protecting the respective positions of the Client and the Quantity Surveyor can be implemented.

6 Copyright

6.1 The copyright in all documents prepared by the Quantity Surveyor in providing the services shall remain the property of the Quantity Surveyor. Subject to payment by the Client of the fees properly due to the Quantity Surveyor under this Agreement the Quantity Surveyor grants to the Client an irrevocable non-exclusive royalty-free licence to copy and use the documents for any purpose related to the project.

6.2 The Quantity Surveyor shall not be liable for any use of the documents for any purpose other than that for which they were prepared and provided by the Quantity Surveyor.

7 *Warranties*

7.1 As and when requested by the Client the Quantity Surveyor shall provide the collateral warranties required under Clause 10 of the Form of Enquiry, provided insurance cover is available in accordance with Clause 5 above.

8 *Suspension and termination*

8.1 The Client may suspend performance by the Quantity Surveyor of all or any of the services by giving seven days' written notice to the Quantity Surveyor. If the services have been suspended for a period of more than twelve months either party may terminate the Agreement, by giving written notice to that effect.

8.2 The Client may terminate the appointment of the Quantity Surveyor under this Agreement by giving seven days' written notice to the Quantity Surveyor.

8.3 Where the services have been suspended by the Client and the Agreement has not been terminated, the Client may, by giving reasonable written notice to the Quantity Surveyor, require the Quantity Surveyor to resume the performance of the services.

8.4 If the Client materially breaches its obligations under this Agreement the Quantity Surveyor may serve on the Client a notice specifying the breach and requiring its remedy within twenty-eight days, and if the Client thereafter fails to remedy that breach within that period the Quantity Surveyor may terminate this Agreement by given written notice to the Client.

8.5 If either party:

- commits an act of bankruptcy or has a receiving or administrative order made against it, and/or
- goes into liquidation, and/or
- becomes insolvent, and/or
- makes any arrangement with its creditors

the other may suspend performance of the services or may terminate the appointment by giving written notice to the Client.

8.6 These rights are in addition to those granted to the Quantity Surveyor under Clause 4 above.

9 *Consequences of suspension and termination*

9.1 If performance of the services has been suspended under Clause 4 or Clause 8 above or the Agreement has been terminated pursuant to the provisions of Clause 8 above:

(a) the Client shall pay the Quantity Surveyor any instalments of the fees due to the Quantity Surveyor up to the date of suspension or termination together with a fair and reasonable proportion of the next following instalment commensurate with the services performed by the Quantity Surveyor.

(b) unless the Agreement has been terminated by the Client because of a material breach by the Quantity Surveyor the Client shall pay the Quantity Surveyor within twenty-eight days of written demand the consequential costs necessarily incurred as a result of the suspension or termination.

9.2 Termination of the Agreement shall be without prejudice to the rights and remedies of the parties.

10 Complaints

10.1 In the event that the Client has a complaint in respect of the performance of the Quantity Surveyor's services under this Agreement, without prejudice to any other remedy available under the Agreement, he shall be entitled to have access to the complaints handling procedure maintained by the Quantity Surveyor, written copies of which should be available on request from the Quantity Surveyor.

11 Disputes

11.1 If a dispute arises out of this Agreement the Client and the Quantity Surveyor shall attempt to agree a settlement in good faith. The internal complaints procedure mentioned in Clause 8.1 of Selection and Appointment Advice should facilitate this for disputes less than £50,000.

11.2 If the dispute is not thus resolved either the Client or the Quantity Surveyor may at any time give notice to the other in writing that he wishes to refer the dispute to an adjudicator, provided the contract is in writing and/or is not with a residential occupier. The person who is to act as the adjudicator shall be agreed between the Client and Quantity Surveyor within two days of such notice having been given or, failing agreement, be a person appointed by the President or Vice-President of the Chartered Institute of Arbitrators within five days of such notice having been given. The referring party shall refer the dispute in writing to the adjudicator within seven days of such notice having been given.

11.3 The adjudication shall be conducted in accordance with the Construction Industry Council Model Adjudication Procedures current at the time of entering into this Agreement. Clause 30 of the Construction Industry Council Model Adjudication Procedures shall be amended to add the following sentence:

'No party shall be entitled to raise any right of set-off, counterclaim and/or abatement in connection with any enforcement proceedings.'

11.4 The adjudicator shall act impartially and may take the initiative in ascertaining the facts and the law

11.5 The adjudicator shall reach a decision:

(a) within twenty-eight days of the referral of the dispute to the adjudicator, or
(b) within forty-two days of the referral of the dispute to the adjudicator if the referring party so consents, or
(c) in a period exceeding twenty-eight days from referral of the dispute to the adjudicator as the Client and the Quantity Surveyor may agree after such referral.

11.6 The adjudicator is not liable for anything he does or omits to do in the discharge or purported discharge of his functions as adjudicator unless the act or omission is in bad faith. Any employee or agent of the adjudicator shall be similarly protected from liability.

11.7 The decision of the adjudicator shall, subject to the provisions of Clauses 11.8 and 11.9 below, be binding until the dispute is finally determined by arbitration either under the contract or as part of the Quantity Surveyor's internal complaints procedure for disputes less than £50,000.

11.8 The Client and the Quantity Surveyor may agree to accept the decision of the adjudicator as finally determining the dispute.

11.9 If the Client or the Quantity Surveyor is dissatisfied with the decision of the adjudicator then:

(a) the dispute may be determined by agreement between the parties, or
(b) the dispute may be referred at the instance of either of the parties to be determined by an arbitrator in accordance with Clause 12 below.

12 Arbitration

12.1 Any dispute arising under this Agreement, including those for more than £50,000 and/or those where adjudication would not apply, may be referred at the instance of either of the parties to be determined by an arbitrator. The person who is to act as an arbitrator shall be agreed between the parties within twenty-eight days of the one giving written notice of his wish to refer the decision to an arbitrator or, failing agreement at the end of that period, shall be a person appointed by the President or Vice-president of the Chartered Institute of Arbitrators at the instance of either party. The arbitration shall be conducted in accordance with the Construction Industry Model Arbitration Rules current at the time of entering into this Agreement.

13 Liability

13.1 The liability of the Quantity Surveyor shall be limited to such sum as it would be just and equitable for the Quantity Surveyor to pay having regard to the extent of the responsibility of the Quantity Surveyor for the loss or damage suffered on the basis that all other consultants, the contractor and any subcontractors who have a liability shall be deemed to have provided contractual undertakings to the Client on terms no less onerous than those applying in the case of this Agreement and shall be deemed to have paid to the Client such sums as it would be just and equitable for them to pay having regard to the extent of their responsibility for such loss or damage.

13.2 The liability of the Quantity Surveyor shall be limited to the amount of the professional indemnity insurance required by virtue of Clause 5.1 above.

13.3 No action or proceedings for any breach of this Agreement shall be commenced by either party after the expiry of the period of limitation (specified in Clause 9 of the Form of Enquiry).

14 Notice

14.1 Any notice to be given under this Agreement shall be in writing and delivered by hand or sent by recorded delivery post to the party at the address shown in this Agreement or to such an address as the other party may have specified from time to time by written notice to the other.

14.2 Such notice shall be deemed to have been received on the day of delivery if delivered by hand and otherwise on the next working day.

14.3 Where under this Agreement an act is required to be completed within a specified period of days after or from a specified date, the period shall begin immediately after that date. Where the period would include a day which is Christmas Day, Good Friday or a day which under the Banking and Financial Dealings Act 1971 is a bank holiday that day shall be excluded.

Table of authorities

Page numbers listed in bold

Table of statutes and statutory instruments

Page numbers listed in bold

Index